AGENT OF
DEMOCRACY

Higher Education and
the HEX Journey

D1446187

Agent of Democracy: Higher Education and the HEX Journey is published by Kettering Foundation Press. The interpretations and conclusions contained in this book represent the views of the authors. They do not necessarily reflect the views of the Charles F. Kettering Foundation, its directors, or its officers.

For information about permission to reproduce selections from this book, write to:

Permissions
Kettering Foundation Press
200 Commons Road
Dayton, Ohio 45459

This book is printed on acid-free paper.

First edition, 2008

Manufactured in the United States of America

ISBN: 978-0-923993-27-6
Library of Congress Control Number: 2007942208

Contents

Introduction
Why This Book?

At a Kettering Foundation 1998 seminar on the professions and public life, William Sullivan warned that:

> Today's discourse about education … is described primarily as a vehicle for individual advance. But there is something called common goods, or public goods, that are worth achieving too, because without them our particular goods are not stable or secure.

Like Sullivan, Kettering has a longstanding concern that the professional mind-set prevailing in higher education ignores the "common goods" that only democratic self-rule can provide. Why? The professional mind-set is profoundly antidemocratic when presuming that one's specialized knowledge and experience is a sufficient substitute for a democratic process of participating equals. Although there are currently many higher education experiments in which the public sets the agenda for research and actually conducts much of the work, there are still too many projects ostensibly done for the public with nothing to be done by the public. When colleges and universities collaborate with the staff of civic organizations, it is often just professional to professional even though the rhetoric is that they are "engaging communities."

Sullivan's warning and Kettering's concern are similar to Tocqueville's early caution about "administrative despotism [which] does not destroy anything but prevents much from being born" and Dewey's later observation that hierarchical and narrow specialization is "inimical to the development of a responsibly democratic polity and the full development of individual personality."

How then can the academy with such a mind-set and its preoccupation with hustling prospective students and chasing after academic luminaries be of any help in renewing democratic practices? As one academic insider recently noted:

> It seems to me to be an incredible proposition for faculty to be attempting to convince community members that they can help lead them to more active, participative and democratic processes that are not in effective practice on their own campuses.

Kettering, however, has never given up on the potential of those in the academy to put aside the professional mind-set and play a constructive role in renewing democratic practices in which there is a place for everyone. Kettering created the *Higher Education Exchange (HEX)* in 1994 as a place of exchange among those across the country already exploring the linkages between higher education and democracy. Kettering wanted to know what institutions are doing to assist in the work a sovereign public must do, what faculty are doing with citizens to coproduce new knowledge, and how students are learning the skills and habits of democratic self-rule.

Now in 2007, this book looks back at what Kettering and *HEX* have learned and looks forward to the prospects for the academy being a better ally, less the adversary, of democracy.

How the Book Is Organized

Three years ago David Brown, coeditor of *HEX*, wrote "Talking the Walk: Making Sense of *HEX* (1994-2004)," recounting how *HEX* got started with a "nascent conversation" among:

> educators who could learn from each other … where everyone should have access and opportunities to improve what they find—much like what good teaching and research are about, or a healthy democracy for that matter, which is the Kettering Foundation's central concern.

Soon after, we asked eight of those educators to fashion a book that explores the linkages between higher education and a "healthy democracy" that have been forged and those that offer some promise. We were sorry we could not include the other distinctive voices, a hundred or more, who have contributed to *HEX* since 1994. Nonetheless, those who came together had a range of experience and points of view that we thought were representative of what we call "the *HEX* years."

The book is rooted in what these eight educators have written for *HEX* over the years, and we have salted each chapter with quotes from their prior contributions. We did not want, however, a stew of their previous writings, but instead new pieces informed by their current work and the conversations they shared at Kettering workshops over the two years the book was in development. At the workshops, they used a deliberative process, not for the sake of compromise or consensus but knowing that together they could fashion a richer understanding of what higher education can do to revitalize democratic practices. Everyone understood that such an exchange helped curb any pretensions that someone could somehow get things "right" before engaging others in the ongoing narrative that developed. As veterans of the academic scene, no one had any illusions that there would be agreement and some were puzzled by being paired up in chapters, but we stuck with it so that differing views coexist in the book, just as they did in the workshop conversations they shared.

Chapter One—The Landscape of Higher Education

To start things off, we asked Peter Levine, research scholar and director of the Center for Information and Research on Civic Learning and Engagement at the University of Maryland, to describe from his vantage point what has been going on in higher education since Kettering first published *HEX*, or what David Mathews referred to as the "landscape."

Of course, when any group of people views a landscape, each person may see and remember different highlights. For Levine, what first distinguished the *HEX* years was the engagement of what he calls "Boomer faculty," a generation shaped by the tumultuous 60s and 70s, with Generation X and their "rejection of formal politics." The engagement of these two generations turned them to various forms of voluntary public work, which included service learning, deliberation, public scholarship, and using diversity to "expand the cultural commons." Levine sees a greater interest in formal politics with the coming of the Millennial Generation, shaped by the events of 9/11, but he notes that these three intersecting generations are all committed to the "open-endedness" of "democratic participation, diversity, consensus building, and constructive problem-solving … values [that] have deep roots in American political history."

Knowing that Levine could not provide a comprehensive picture of the higher education landscape, at least not in one opening chapter, we asked Mary Stanley, an independent scholar, formerly at Syracuse University, to weigh in with her view, knowing that it was likely to be very different from Levine's. He himself pointed out in a *HEX* 2004 interview that "the culture of American universities is not uniform, rather it is passionately contested." That is certainly true in the chapter that he and Stanley share.

As Stanley sees it, Levine and others have boarded "the democracy train," while ignoring the market-driven "neoliberal train that seems to be gathering the whole of humanity, forcing its passengers to rush ever faster to a temporal and spatial world that just might destroy our capacity for community." For Stanley, globalization spares no one, including those who labor in academia, from the consequences of unbridled capitalism.

She argues that too many in higher education are too much the unwitting allies of globalization when they retreat into civil society. She fears that "the larger political economy becomes the weather; out there, not of us. Or the 'thing' gentleman and ladies don't discuss." For Stanley, Kettering and her *HEX* colleagues are obviously part of that polite company.

She thinks that higher education institutions must do more than just acknowledge those who share her dissenting view. They should, given Levine's stress on open-endedness, make room for the consideration of macro changes to deal with "the conundrums, contradictions and tensions globalization brings to all institutional sectors, including their own." Although Stanley is far from satisfied, she does not totally despair. For her, the "world-spanning, neoliberal political economy so vast and seemingly uncontrollable, is a human creation, was once otherwise and could be different."

Chapter Two—The Civic Roots of Higher Education

We asked Claire Snyder, associate professor of political theory and director of academics for the higher education program at

George Mason University, to reflect on a piece she had written for *HEX* in 1998 providing an important, but neglected, story about the "civic roots" of higher education. We agreed that there are far too many in academia who are ignorant of such roots. Since it is difficult to get more than lip service to the work of democracy in the precincts of higher education, Snyder's work has been indispensable and she continues to explore the past and present civic dimensions in the piece that she has written for the book.

Although Snyder acknowledges higher education has had "multiple understandings" of a "civic mission," she "privileges" the "republican version of civic" over the "liberal individualistic" version in which "the liberal citizen has individual rights but few duties." But because the liberal version currently prevails, she questions the current adequacy of higher education's civic mission. "If democratic citizenship involves acting collectively to achieve common goals, then what does higher education need to do to prepare citizens for that task?" She remains uncertain that higher education will "play its historic role in helping democracy work as it should."

Chapter Three—Public Work

We wanted to include important perspectives that have emerged from *HEX*, and Harry Boyte, codirector of the Center for Democracy and Citizenship at the University of Minnesota, was certainly the obvious choice as far as "public work" is concerned. David Brown had just completed an interview with Adam Weinberg, then Dean of the College at Colgate, and Weinberg reminded him of how much Boyte's concept of public work had influenced his work with students at Colgate. As Boyte puts it:

> Democracy is, in fact, a kind of work. Its labors occur in multiple sites, enlist multiple talents in addressing public problems, and result in multiple forms of common wealth. The public works of democracy create an environment of equal respect.

So Boyte's piece and Weinberg's interview, which follows it, combine that concept with an excellent story about how one institution put public work to work, so to speak.

Boyte welcomed the opportunity for "updating and new thoughts," given the intellectual and experimental ground that he had covered since David Brown's *HEX* interview with him in 2000. In tying the threads together, Boyte takes aim at "technocratic politics—domination by experts removed from a common civic life—[that] has spread throughout contemporary society like a silent disease." The Boyte "voice" on public work remains at the center of what Kettering and *HEX* are about—*democracy* is a verb.

Chapter Four—Public Scholarship

We asked Scott Peters, associate professor of education at Cornell University, who has been so prominent in *HEX* journals helping to develop the perspective of "public scholarship," to share his ongoing research of the new connections that land-grant colleges and universities have been forging with the public. Peters' piece anchors the chapter, which also includes Jeremy Cohen's story of the public scholarship of faculty and students at Penn State.

In his piece, Peters responds to a question posed by Noëlle McAfee, another contributor to the book, "what kind of relationship should there be between the academy and the public?" Looking back, Peters sees the importance of the agriculture extension work of the land-grant system. Looking ahead, however, he sees a "civic conception of academic professionalism" more tenuous. After conducting extensive interviews, both individual and focus group, with current land-grant faculty engaged with the public, Peters found that these "remarkably positive people" do not see their work "valued, supported, or pursued by most of their academic peers." And so he concludes that such scholars face the task of *reconstructing* the democratic tradition of public scholarship in the land-grant system. Can they succeed?

Cohen, professor of communication and associate vice president and senior associate dean for undergraduate education at Penn State University, hardened by academic experience but with an infectious idealism nonetheless, was the subject of a *HEX* interview in 2005 and told about the ongoing story of public scholarship at Penn State. So we asked him to advance that narrative by contributing to the *HEX* book underway, and he readily agreed, seeing his work with Kettering as contributing to his work and commitment at Penn State.

In his piece, Cohen ranges beyond the Penn State story to put it in the larger context of American constitutional history and argues for "purposeful democratic learning," that is, "learning to be democratic." He thinks, "We have failed as educators to fully grasp the fact that nothing about democracy, not its theory and certainly not its practice, is hard wired into anyone." The story then at Penn State seeks to remedy this "failure."

Chapter Five—Public Making

There was no better person to discuss democratic deliberation than Noëlle McAfee, visiting associate professor of philosophy at George Mason University, who has worked closely with Kettering and others to make such a practice take hold in various jurisdictions. In fact, having the book's contributors deliberate together in workshops over two years could have been McAfee's idea in the first place. We were sure that we needed her for such an undertaking, which, to borrow David Mathews' observation about democracy itself, was to be "more a journey than a destination."

For the book, we asked McAfee to offer her perspective on the potential of higher education institutions for "public making," or "public building" as some put it. She resisted any "model" for such institutions that has them "organize" others, which can too easily resort to the hierarchical relationship between expert and public. She insisted that only citizens through their own democratic deliberation and public work can become a "public." McAfee believes, however, that academic institutions can be an important "ally" through their "research and teaching with a newfound respect for public work." As she put it at the concluding workshop, "ally" fits her preference for "horizontal" relationships and makes it more "*HEX*ish."

The perspective of public making needed an institutional story to ground it and Doug Challenger, associate professor of sociology at Franklin Pierce University, has certainly lived that perspective in the work of the college allied with the community of Rindge, New

Hampshire. Challenger tells the story of the ups and downs of that civic journey together, and a "pivotal moment" when those in Rindge "realized that they had the answers to their own local problems and had grown to trust deliberative community dialogue as a way to access their own collective wisdom." McAfee's point exactly.

Working with others, Challenger helped to establish the New England Center for Civic Life to serve as a catalyst for other communities and colleges to offer "a fresh approach to politics" through "the work of citizens in grassroot efforts." In taking that journey, it also led Challenger back to his own campus and to a renewed focus of using deliberative dialogue including a "deliberative session" that became a part of the monthly faculty meetings. There is no conclusion to his institutional story. Like others, it continues to evolve.

Chapter Six—Democracy's Megachallenges Revisited

After looking at the academy and what we've learned, in the concluding chapter David Mathews characteristically looks through the other end of the telescope and asks, "What does all the ferment over democracy mean for higher education?"

> The world is struggling with the meaning of democracy as current problems challenge old forms. Questions of where academic institutions will weigh in—and how—are inescapable. The way these questions are answered, knowingly or not, will be the ultimate measure of how accountable colleges and universities are to the public.

For Mathews and all his coauthors here, the book is not meant to conclude the *HEX* years but to extend them by what those both inside and outside the academy do to renew and sustain the practices of democratic self-rule.

—*David Brown*
—*Deborah Witte*

CHAPTER ONE

The Landscape of Higher Education

The Engaged University: A Tale of Two Generations

The Limits of Public Work: A Critical Reflection on the "Engaged University"

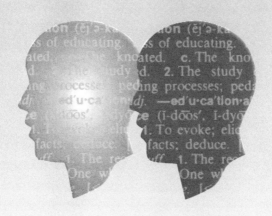

The Engaged University:
A Tale of Two Generations

Peter Levine

The *Higher Education Exchange,* an annual publication devoted to public scholarship, deliberation, and other forms of civic work in colleges and universities, first appeared in 1994. It became a venue for discussing and debating a new set of practices on college campuses, which included service learning, efforts to capitalize on the increasing diversity of students and faculty, community-based scholarship, and experiments with deliberation. Although various, most of these practices shared an important feature: they were open-ended. That is, their organizers did not try to drive participants toward particular views, but instead created opportunities for

> *"Instead of throwing all professors together into a single category . . . I would draw distinctions by discipline, by type of institution and career path, even by age and generation."*
>
> ("The Engaged University: An interview with Peter Levine," *HEX*, 2003.)

discussion and practical experimentation that might lead in unexpected directions. This open-endedness did not imply a lack of ideals or commitments. On the contrary, participants were committed to democratic participation, diversity, consensus building, and constructive problem solving. Those values have deep roots in American political history. I will describe their reemergence since 1994 by telling a story about two interacting generations.

The Theory of Generations

Because human beings are born continuously, a "generation" is a something of a fiction. However, Karl Mannheim argued that most people are forced to develop a stance toward news, issues, and governments when they first encounter the broader world, usually late in adolescence. Thereafter, the psychic cost of reevaluating one's political stance is not worth the price, unless a major event (such as a war or revolution) forces a review. As Mannheim wrote, "even if the rest of one's life consisted in one long process of negation and destruction of the natural world view acquired in youth, the determining influence of these early impressions would still be predominant."

Mannheim's theory implies that a major event will have especially profound and lasting effects on people who are young when it occurs. Such an event can cause people of similar age to coalesce into a generation that has an enduring character. Mannheim called this process of coalescence "entelechy."[1] He developed his theory in the 1920s (influenced by the unmistakable impact of World War I on those born after 1890); but recent statistical evidence supports his theory that people develop lasting civic identities in adolescence.[2]

Boomer Faculty

In 1994, as at all times, several generations were present in American colleges. Faculty and staff born before 1945 were certainly influential and active, as they are today. However, two younger generations were especially relevant to the story that unfolded in the pages of *HEX*.

First, consider the large cohort of professors who had first encountered the public world—and academia—during the Johnson and Nixon administrations. This was a tumultuous time, marked by war, assassinations, social movements, protests, and a sexual revolution. Campuses were at the center of the tumult. Students provided prominent national leaders for all the major social movements of

---

[1] Karl Mannheim, "The Problem of Generations" (1928), available in *Essays on the Sociology of Knowledge*, edited by Paul Kecskemeti (London, 1952), 298.

[2] For a good summary of recent literature, see Constance Flanagan and Lonnie R. Sherrod, "Youth Political Development: An Introduction," *Journal of Social Issues* (Fall 1998). The period between ages 14 and 25 is identified as crucial in R.G. Niemi and M.A. Hepburn, "The Rebirth of Political Socialization," *Perspectives on Political Science*, vol. 24 (1995): 7-16.

the day; most male students were confronted with a powerful political dilemma in the form of the draft; young people experimented with new lifestyles in revolt against their parents' generation; and urban campuses were sites of struggle as many central cities burned. According to data collected by Sarah Soule and Ann Marie Condo from newspaper archives, the United States saw more than twice as many "protest events" per year between 1964 and 1974 than during the 1980s. In 1970, more than half of all protests were initiated by youth (including college students), whereas only 10 to 20 percent had youth leaders in the 1980s.[3] In other words, student and youth protests were an important part of the national political scene in 1970 but were either rare or unnoticed 15 years later.

Thus a large cohort of professors developed their fundamental attitudes toward the world in general, and academia in particular, at a time of political upheaval when colleges and members of their own generation, defined as "students," played a leading role—not only in the United States, but also (and with more consequence) in countries like France, South Korea, and Chile. They came of age conscious of a "generation gap" and prone to see colleges as sites of political opposition, critique, and even revolution. Even 30 years later, half of the Baby Boomer generation agreed that "my age group is unique," compared to [just] 42 percent of the Generation-Xers who followed them.[4]

Between the Boomers' formative years on campus and the appearance of *HEX*, things had calmed down considerably. Some prominent leftist intellectuals had moved to the right. Some had adopted postmodernist theories that, if they were political at all, certainly lacked any political "praxis" (i.e., an answer to Lenin's question, what is to be done?). Some Boomer academics had held

---

[3] Sarah A. Soule and Ann Marie Condo, "Student and Youth Protest in the United States, 1960-1990" (paper presented at the Democracy Collaborative's Spring Research Seminar, University of Maryland, 2005, and cited with permission).

[4] Scott Keeter, Cliff Zukin, Molly Andolina, and Krista Jenkins, "The Civic and Political Health of the Nation: A Generational Portrait" (September 2002), 37, available from the Center for Information and Research on Civic Learning and Engagement (CIRCLE) at http://www.civicyouth.org/research/products/youth_index.htm.

onto their radical values but had become disillusioned with colleges' political potential as most of their students had abandoned sixties-style activism. Some, technically part of the baby boom but in graduate school after 1975, faced what David D. Cooper called "the chronically depressed conditions of an insanely competitive job market," making ends meet by teaching adjunct courses at several institutions and never having the time or power to be active politically.[5]

> *"Intellectuals are also entitled to participate not as professionals but as citizens with personal opinions and interests, just like everyone else's. But when they adopt that role, they must make sure not to claim or imply any special authority."*
>
> ("Public Intellectuals and the Influence of Economics," *HEX*, 2001.)

Finally, some had developed a new perspective that, while still reformist and egalitarian, was increasingly pragmatic, open-ended, and solicitous of institutions, of existing communities, of civic culture, and of public deliberation, regardless of its outcome.

Cooper wrote in *HEX* that he "was bent on nourishing the fragile bond between the inner life and ethical responsibility to work, institution, and community."[6] He contrasted this civic commitment to the standard approach of his academic discipline, which was "abstract, contentious, and theory-driven." Edward Royce could have been describing Cooper when he wrote a *HEX* article about scholars who were not so much interested in "social criticism" as in using "their intellectual capital to inform, educate, and empower ordinary citizens."[7] These people played a central role in *HEX*.

---

[5] David D. Cooper, "Bus Rides and Forks in the Road: The Making of a Public Scholar," *Higher Education Exchange* (2002): 29.

[6] Ibid., 32.

[7] Edward Royce, "The Practice of the Public Intellectual," *Higher Education Exchange* (1999): 26.

The shift that I am describing was ideological. Cooper, Royce, and other contributors to *HEX* made points incompatible with Marxist and postmodernist political theories. They were eager to strengthen and enhance *existing* forms of democratic politics and recover local traditions. They were also inclined to listen to what their fellow citizens were saying, instead of suspecting that other people had been manipulated by capitalism, advertising, or politicians to adopt positions contrary to justice and their own interests. They rejected the "hermeneutics of suspicion," in Paul Ricoeur's phrase.

When *HEX* was founded, less than one in five Americans identified themselves as "liberals" in the National Election Studies poll, compared to 35 to 40 percent who called themselves "conservatives." (That remained the ratio in 2004.) Therefore, academics who held open-ended discussions with their fellow Americans had to listen to a lot of arguments and premises associated with the political right. Professors who believed in open-ended deliberation might disagree with these conservative opinions, but they couldn't dismiss them or bypass them. The fundamental premise of deliberative politics is that one ought to take other people's beliefs and opinions seriously and treat them with respect. If average Americans deserved to be listened to, and if a plurality voted for conservative politicians and causes, then the ascendancy of the right could not be dismissed as the result of nefarious tactics by elites (e.g., campaign donations, media manipulation, and the like.) It had to be treated as a legitimate popular movement and the authentic point from which many Americans *entered* conversations.

> *"I think it should be pointed out that the culture of American universities is not uniform; rather, it is passionately contested."*
>
> ("What Is 'Public' About What Academics Do?: An exchange with Robert Kingston and Peter Levine," *HEX*, 2004.)

Nevertheless, the new civic politics was not itself right-of-center, or moderate, or otherwise easy to categorize ideologically.

Some proponents thought that civic engagement and dialogue might unleash radical and unpredictable social change; new political vistas would open. Some believed that the political equality and respect intrinsic in truly open-ended public deliberation was more radical than the economic redistribution promised by an activist state.

Gen-X Students

In 1994, when many professors were Boomers, their students predominantly belonged to Generation X (born between 1965 and 1984). A typical undergraduate of that time had begun to pay attention to the public world during the relatively uneventful administrations of George H. W. Bush and Bill Clinton. Members of Gen X formed a relatively small cohort, raised in the shadow of the much more numerous Boomers, and they had the weakest sense of their own distinctness as a generation. In fact, no entelechy had occurred during their formative years. However, the X-ers shared a sense that they had arrived too late for the dramatic events of 1965 to 1975, yet they lived with the consequences of their parents' choices. Further, they were marked by rising economic anxiety and a belief that their individual performance in school would have profound effects on their economic futures. For "high-performing" students, including those who were female or people of color, some new opportunities seemed to have opened up. But the obverse of opportunity was risk. Students believed that they stood alone in the economy, unable to fall back on unions, neighborhoods, or even intact families. Especially after the recession of the early 1990s, higher education seemed the indispensable key to security. The economic value of college, rather than its potential for social change, was its most salient feature for students and their parents alike.[8]

The annual survey of incoming first-year college students conducted by the Higher Education Research Institute (HERI)

---

8 See Lewis A. Friedland and Shauna Morimoto, "The Changing Lifeworld of Young People: Risk, Resume-Padding, and Civic Engagement," (CIRCLE Working Paper number 40, September 2005).

reveals significant changes between 1970 and 1994. In 1970, seventy-nine percent of the entering freshmen identified "developing a meaningful philosophy of life" as an important goal. By 1994, that was a choice of just 46 percent. The trend line for "becoming well off financially" moved in just the opposite direction: 36 percent identified it as a major goal in 1970, compared to 72 percent of the Gen-X freshmen in 1994.

Leftist students (2.2 percent of freshmen in the 1994 HERI sample) deserve special consideration, because in my experience they provided a disproportionate percentage of campus activists, leaders of student associations, and partners for the Boomer professors who were working on public projects in the 1990s. These young leftists were different from earlier generations of progressive /activist students, precisely because their formative experiences had occurred during the Clinton administration. Before the 1992 election, most activist students of the left had favored "community service" if (and only if) it sensitized people to problems like poverty and racism and led to political action. They preferred voting and fundamental change through state action, fearing that service might become an end in itself or a palliative. These were some of the explicit conclusions of a Wingspread summit on service that I attended in 1988 as a student. Thirteen years later, Campus Compact brought a new group of activist undergraduates (including some conservatives) to Wingspread to discuss civic engagement. These students, summarizing the experience of the 1990s, said:

> For the most part, we are frustrated with conventional politics, viewing it as inaccessible. [However,] while we are disillusioned with conventional politics (and therefore most forms of political activity), we are deeply involved in civic issues through non-traditional forms of engagement. We are neither apathetic nor disengaged. In fact, what many perceive as disengagement may actually be a conscious choice; for example, a few of us … actively avoided voting, not wanting to participate in what some of us view as a deeply flawed electoral process.… While we still hope to be able to participate in our political system effectively through

traditional means, service is a viable and preferable
(if not superior) alternative at this time.[9]

I suspect that a major reason for this rejection of formal politics
was the failure of the Clinton administration to achieve goals prized
by leftist students, following the built-up hopes of the Reagan and
Bush years. The spike in youth voting in 1992 gave way to a substantial turnout decline in 1996 and 2000. However, the rate of student
volunteering increased just as turnout fell. As Bill Galston and I
wrote in 1997:

> Citizens—particularly the youngest—seem to be
> shifting their preferred civic involvement from offi-
> cial politics to the voluntary sector. If so, the classic
> Tocquevillian thesis would have to be modified: local
> civic life, far from acting as a school for wider political
> involvement, may increasingly serve as a refuge from
> (and alternative to) it. The consequences for the future
> of our democracy could be significant.[10]

In the 1990s, disillusioned leftists could find common ground
with some conservative and libertarian youth who were equally
skeptical about state action, and equally optimistic about voluntary
work in the nonprofit sector. Activist students of the right and left
developed a non-state-centered theory of politics and social change.
These young proponents of "service politics"—optimistic about
direct work with human beings in need, concerned and self-critical
about personal attitudes and behaviors, relatively skilled at interactions with people different from themselves, and disillusioned
with formal politics—encountered a group of academics whose own
thinking had moved in compatible directions.

---

[9] "The New Student Politics: The Wingspread Statement on Student Civic Engagement" (2002), available at http://www.actionforchange.org/getinformed/nsp-
download.html. Discussed at length in David D. Cooper, "Education for Democracy:
A Conversation in Two Keys," *Higher Education Exchange* (2004): 30-43.

[10] William A. Galston and Peter Levine, "America's Civic Condition: A Glance
at the Evidence," *The Brookings Review*, vol. 15, no. 4 (Fall 1997): 26. This article
is reprinted in *Community Works: The Revival of Civil Society in America*, ed. E.J.
Dionne Jr. (Washington D.C.: Brookings Institution Press, 1998), 30-36.

New Scholarly Attention to "the Public"

During the 1980s and early 1990s, many scholars had been paying renewed attention to *civil society*: voluntary associations and the norms of membership and trust that accompany them. In Marxist thought, "civil society" is irrelevant to history, a mere symptom of the underlying economic order. But it was civil society that defeated Leninist states in Russia and Eastern Europe. It was also within civil society that the women's movement and other revolutionary social forces arose in the West and achieved major victories. Meanwhile, the *quality* of civil society in a nation or a neighborhood seemed to explain its economic well-being, political resiliency, and even the quality of its schools.

A large body of literature, including influential works by James Coleman in sociology; Robert Putnam in political science; James C. Scott in anthropology; and Jean Cohen, Andrew Arato, and Joshua Cohen in political theory, drew attention to the importance of civil society and the public's role in a democracy. As a result of this literature, older authors, such as John Dewey and Jane Addams, enjoyed a renaissance.[11]

> *"Now I work mainly on civic education at the kindergarten to twelfth grade level, hoping that young people can be made more interested in walking through any doors to civic engagement."*
>
> ("What is 'Public' About What Academics Do?: An exchange with Robert Kingston and Peter Levine," *HEX*, 2004.)

A related intellectual development was a renewed concern with *deliberation*. In the 1970s, two of the most influential political philosophers in the world, the American John Rawls and the German Jürgen Habermas, had argued that justice could not be determined by any abstract methodology, such as utilitarianism, but had to be discovered by people reasoning together. For people who

---

[11] See, for instance, Jay Rosen's article, "Making Things More Public: On the Political Responsibility of the Media Intellectual," *Higher Education Exchange* (1995): 43-55.

use Deweyan vocabulary, the *public* is the population when it deliberates and acts on common concerns. As Maria Farland noted in *HEX*:

> Despite the enormous diversity of approaches that characterize the new public mindedness among today's academic professionals, there is ample evidence that "the public" has emerged as a common concern in fields as diverse as urban planning and English literature.[12]

To prize civil society and deliberation is to take a political stance that is open-ended about outcomes, but strongly committed to values like participation, equity in discussion, freedom of speech, civility, and problem solving.

New Forms of Public Work

When Boomer intellectuals, increasingly focused on public deliberation and civil society, encountered young people who were disillusioned with formal, state-centered politics (but optimistic about the potential of "service"), the two generations began to experiment with innovative forms of voluntary public work that exemplified their new theories of citizen-centered deliberative democracy.

The most prevalent example was *service learning*, defined as an intentional combination of community service with reflection on the same issue or topic. The phrase seems to have been coined in 1967.[13] By then, there was already a rich history of such work, including the Settlement House movement, the Appalachian Folk Schools (of which Highlander was most famous), and the Civilian Conservation Corps, which provided formal civic education programs connected to service work.[14] However, service learning grew and was institutionalized rapidly in higher education during the 1980s and 1990s, partly

---

[12] Maria Farland, "Academic Professionalism and the New Public Mindedness," *Higher Education Exchange* (1996): 54.

[13] Peter Titlebaum, Gabrielle Williamson, Corinne Daprano, Janine Baer, and Jayne Brahler, "The Annotated History of Service-Learning: 1862-2002" at http://www.servicelearning.org/welcome_to_service-learning/history/index.php (accessed August 8, 2007).

[14] Melissa Bass, "National Service in America: Policy (Dis)Connections Over Time" (CIRCLE Working Paper 11) and "Civic Education through National Service" (CIRCLE Working Paper 12).

thanks to several energetic new advocacy organizations: the Campus Opportunity Outreach League, or COOL (founded in 1984), Campus Compact (1985), and Youth Service America (1986). The federal government assisted by creating the Points of Light Foundation, passing the National and Community Service Act of 1990, and launching the Corporation for National Service in 1993.

In colleges and universities, service learning is now very common and various. In my view, the best examples are true collaborations among students, professors, and community members; they have a political dimension (that is, they organize people to tackle fundamental problems collectively); they combine deliberation with concrete action; and they are connected to "teaching and learning, research, and the dissemination of knowledge"—the goals that, as Deborah Hirsch wrote in *HEX*, "drive the university."[15] Good service learning gives students the authority to choose their own problems and responses. The professor's stance is open-ended. Much service learning fails to meet these criteria, but the movement is full of energy and innovation.

A second example of the new public work was *concrete experimentation with deliberation*, as exemplified by National Issues Forums, Study Circles, Deliberative Polls, and Citizens' Juries. Some of these experiments originated in universities. For instance, the Center for Deliberative Polling at the University of Texas organized and studied deliberative exercises. In other cases, independent groups, such as the National Issues Forums network and the Study Circles Resource Center, led the experiments, but their reflective practitioners engaged in dialogues with academics. And sometimes, higher education was the site or the topic of public deliberation. *HEX* articles described forums and other deliberative exercises conducted at Virginia Tech, Texas A&M, and Franklin Pierce University.[16] In the 1998 edition,

---

[15] Deborah Hirsch, "An Agenda for Involving Faculty in Service," *Higher Education Exchange* (1997): 35.

[16] D. Conor Seyle, "NIF at A&M," *Higher Education Exchange* (2000): 52-58; Douglas Challenger, "The College as Citizen: One College Evolves through the Work of Public Deliberation," *Higher Education Exchange* (2000): 68-81; Anne Wolford, Larkin Dudley, and Diane Zahm, "Supporting the Mission of a Land Grant University and Cooperate Extension," *Higher Education Exchange* (2002): 72-80.

Susanna Finnell described a series of deliberations about the costs and benefits of college education, organized by the National Collegiate Honors Council.[17]

At Wake Forest, the Democracy Fellows are students who participate in and organize deliberations throughout their four-year undergraduate careers. A rigorous study with a control group found that the Democracy Fellows gained sophistication about politics, efficacy, and an interest in political participation in contrast to standard volunteering.[18] Some institutions have experimented with larger-scale deliberations that take advantage of their research capacities and technical infrastructure, as well as their students' service. For example, the University of California, San Diego, has launched "San Diego Dialogue," an elaborate public deliberation about economic development, which includes citizens of both San Diego and Tijuana and is regularly fed by timely academic research.[19]

A simultaneous and related development was the growth of *practical public scholarship*, the theme of the 1996 edition of *HEX*. It was not a novel idea in the 1990s to conduct research in partnership with lay people. To name one earlier example, Jane Addams had written her enormously influential works of social analysis by working with her own Chicago neighbors, whom she treated as peers and fellow investigators. However, in his 1996 *HEX* article, William Sullivan argued that a different conception of scholarship dominated after the Second World War. This was the idea that experts "'solved problems' by bringing the latest technical knowledge to bear on matters which, it has been widely presumed, the public as a whole was too limited to understand, much less address."[20] After World War

---

[17] Susanna Finnell, "Higher Education: Teaching and the Deliberative Process," *Higher Education Exchange* (1998): 46-53.

[18] Katy J. Harriger and Jill J. McMillan, *Speaking of Politics: Preparing College Students for Democratic Dialogue* (Dayton, OH: Kettering Foundation Press, 2007).

[19] Mathew Hartley and Elizabeth L. Hollander, "The Elusive Ideal: Civic Learning and Higher Education," in *The Public Schools*, eds. Susan Fuhrman and Marvin Lazerson (New York: Oxford University Press, 2005), 267.

[20] William M. Sullivan, "The Public Intellectual as Transgressor," *Higher Education Exchange* (1996): 20.

II, academics were impressed (sometimes justifiably) by detached and scientific methods, such as large-scale survey research and controlled experiments.

By the 1990s, there were evident countertrends, among them the growth of ethnographic methods. Ethnography had been founded by anthropologists like Bronislaw Malinwoski and Margaret Mead, who lived for substantial periods immersed in distant cultures and used local people as informants. By the 1990s, ethnographic methods were widely employed in American contexts, even to understand the academy itself. A "hallmark" of "ethnography is its commitment to accurate reflection of the views and perspectives of the participants in the research"; this requires close and respectful interaction with lay people.[21] In *HEX*, Scott Peters described the Teen Assessment Project (TAP) in Wisconsin, which "provides a means for communities to collaborate with extension educators and university faculty in conducting their own research on the needs and problems faced by adolescents."[22] This was an example of many such projects across the country.[23]

Jay Rosen's work with practical journalists represented a different way of developing new knowledge and ideas in collaboration with nonacademics: in this case, professionals. Rosen explained that he began by thinking about Michael Sandel's famous line, "When politics goes well, we can know a good in common that we cannot know alone." But what does it mean for politics to "go well"? "That's a question that no scholar … can answer alone, or in conversation with other academics." The answer, Rosen argued in *HEX*, "can only be found by creating a space for

---

[21] Margaret D. LeCompte and Jean J. Schensul, *Ethnographer's Toolkit, vol. 1: Designing & Conducting Ethnographic Research* (Walnut Creek, CA: Altamira/Sage Publications, 1999), 12.

[22] Scott J. Peters, "Public Scholarship and the Land-Grant Idea," *Higher Education Exchange* (1997): 55-56.

[23] Cf. the University of Kentucky's partnership with the Public Life Foundation Organization, described by Douglas Scutchfield, Carol Ireson, and Laura Hall in "Bringing Democracy to Health Care: A University-Community Partnership," *Higher Education Exchange* (2004): 55-63.

reflection and discussion within a profession struggling to find a better public ethic."[24]

A final important development in the 1980s and 1990s was work that capitalized on *diversity as an asset*. Indeed, the first two editions of *HEX* were mainly devoted to the controversy over diversity, multiculturalism, and "political correctness" versus some notion of a Western educational canon. For instance, on the first page of the very first *HEX* article, Carlos E. Cortés observed that the "United States has been wracked by a History War" since the 1960s. Struggles over the past had grown increasingly contentious, he argued, because the country had undergone a "Diversity Revolution." He noted that "multicultural research, teaching, and engagement" had "moved from the margins to center stage" during the previous decade, provoking a powerful reaction.[25] In the same issue, Eric Liu (then in his early 20s) observed that his own generation had:

> assiduously read the signals sent out by our public institutions. Be separate. Ask for more. Classify yourselves and stand in line for what is rightly yours.... On the other side of the spectrum, young neoconservatives have delighted in exposing the follies of the politically correct.[26]

Liu's generational interpretation rings true for me, and I would cite a particular event as formative. In 1978, four members of the Supreme Court had ruled that affirmative action was unconstitutional. Four members had supported it as a way to address discrimination and reallocate scarce goods (such as places in college) to disadvantaged groups. The swing vote was Justice Powell's; he argued that affirmative action was permissible only to promote diversity, which in turn could enhance the "robust exchange of ideas," which was a goal "of paramount importance in the fulfillment of [a university's] mission."[27]

---

[24] David Brown, "Public Scholarship: An interview with Jay Rosen," *Higher Education Exchange* (1996): 30.

[25] Carlos E. Cortés, "Backing into the Future: Columbus, Cleopatra, Custer & the Diversity Revolution," *Higher Education Exchange* (1994): 6-8.

[26] Eric Liu, "Shredding the Race Card," *Higher Education Exchange* (1994): 21.

[27] *University of California Regents v. Bakke*, 438 U.S. 265 (1978).

Because Powell's opinion was the law of the land after 1978, and because there were good substantive reasons for it, many colleges and universities began to see affirmative action (broadly defined as any effort to encourage the participation of women and minorities) as essential to their scholarly and educational missions. Meanwhile, surveys found that young people increasingly saw racial diversity as an asset. As Liu noted, "the twentysomething generation is still key, as confused as we may be now. We are the first American generation to have been born in an integrated society, and we are accustomed to more race-mixing than any generation before us."[28]

If there is a common theme to the 13 articles on diversity in the 1994 and 1995 *HEX* issues, it is the search for a positive vision. Often, multiculturalism has a consumerist feel. One assumes that there is a finite supply of cultural goods, each marked with a gender and ethnic tag; the question is how much of students' finite time should be spent consuming "Western" products, versus works of their own choice, versus assigned works by previously excluded groups. I see the early *HEX* authors as struggling for a positive, "win-win" vision in which new generations can not merely consume but also create works that expand the cultural commons, either by combining multiple cultural influences (see John Lahr's review of Anna Deveare Smith in the inaugural *HEX*), or by creating cultural groups on campus that give students a sense that they "matter" (as Daryl G. Smith argued), or by adding "new voices along with the old" (as Cortés recommended).

When students are encouraged to create culturally diverse products and contribute them to the commons, they join a tradition of democratic activism that connects politics closely to culture and sees citizens as creators. As Harry Boyte shows in this volume, cultural politics was the tradition of Hull House in the 1890s, the Popular Front in the 1930s, and the Freedom Movement in the 1960s. It remains essential in some contemporary community organizing work, especially that of the Industrial Areas Foundation and the

---

[28] Liu, "Shredding the Race Card," 22.

PICO and Gamaliel networks. It is not, however, fully compatible with a view of politics that puts economic injustice at the center and emphasizes reforms in state policy. Compared to an economic-injustice model, cultural politics is more respectful of actually existing cultural traditions, more optimistic about people's capacity to create (even under current conditions), and more likely to balance cultural values against economic ones.

In 2003, the Supreme Court upheld affirmative action as constitutional if it enhanced the mission of a university (thus converting Powell's lone opinion into a 5-4 majority). The *Michigan* decision was much influenced by supportive testimony from numerous universities and by experiences with creative diversity during the 1980s and 1990s.

Recent Generational Change

I have described the developments in public scholarship recorded in *HEX* as the fruitful result of an encounter between Boomer academics and students born after 1965. Since 1994, however, most Gen-X college students have moved on and members of the Millennial Generation have replaced them.

Some of the undergraduates who were engaged in public scholarship, service learning, or deliberation when *HEX* was launched went on to obtain doctorates of their own. While that group included people who became civically engaged professors, many responded to the tight job market by becoming knowledge-workers outside academia. Their pragmatism, enthusiasm for collaborating with lay publics, and resistance to large organizations—all generational traits—encouraged them to work in nonprofits and communities. Maria Farland wrote in *HEX* that these younger PhDs were "going public" by working outside academia, and therefore formed "the vanguard of an exciting professional revolution."

> The scholars of my generation who have chosen to leave academic professionalism as it is narrowly defined within the university's walls … address the public, and public problems, in a language and style that differ significantly from the highly specialized

language of the academic discipline in which they were trained. Many are rooted in a particular community, especially urban communities.… The coming of age of my generation has witnessed the emergence of a population of humanists who see the public conversation as the primary context in which they write, conduct research, and sometimes teach.[29]

As for the new generation that first reached college age in 1993— the Millennials, "Dot-Nets," or "echo-Boomers"—they are another large cohort with a strong sense of a generation gap. Sixty-nine percent believe that their generation is unique.[30] That is the highest rate by far, and it is not simply a result of their being young. (There is no linear relationship between age and strength of generational identity.) Mannheim's theory would suggest that an entelechy has occurred. Indeed, many observers suspect that the Millennials experienced the following formative events. They first encountered the public world during the prosperous and peaceful Clinton years, when government seemed to be shrinking but working well, and opportunities were expanding in the entrepreneurial technology markets. Surveys showed them to be idealistic, tolerant, and committed to volunteer service, but not especially political. Then, on September 11, 2001, they were confronted with a frightening attack that was politically motivated and that prompted (or at least excused) the U.S. government to pass momentous laws, start a war, and increase spending. Politics was unavoidable.

It will take decades for the Millennials to sort out their formative experiences, and they will never be of one mind. The early signs, however, suggest a strong commitment to volunteer service matched by an increased interest in formal politics. During the 2004 presidential campaign, three-quarters of college students said that they discussed politics at least once per week; 47 percent of eligible 18- to 24-year-olds actually voted, up 11 percentage points

---

[29] Maria Farland, "Talking About My Generation: The Public Work of Today's Young Scholars," *Higher Education Exchange* (2000): 59, 64-65.

[30] Keeter et al., "The Civic and Political Health of the Nation."

from 2000 and the highest youth turnout since at least 1992.[31] Although the future is certainly unpredictable, there is a significant chance that the academic innovations of the 1980s and 1990s (especially service learning, public scholarship, diversity work, and deliberation) will become more political—more oriented to fundamental social change —as the Millennials make their mark.

---

[31] Richard Niemi and Michael Hanmer, "College Students in the 2004 Election," CIRCLE Fact Sheet (November 2004); Mark Hugo Lopez, Emily Kirby, and Jared Sagoff, "The Youth Vote 2004 (CIRCLE Working Paper, July 2005).

The Limits of Public Work: A Critical Reflection on the "Engaged University"

Mary Stanley

This chapter is dedicated to the late Manfred Stanley,
dear husband, trusted colleague, and love of my life,
whose own work is my model of humane scholarship.

Peter Levine's tale of two generations of scholars is one framework for introducing the reader to the *Higher Education Exchange*. It's a good analysis of the *whys*, *hows*, and *whos* behind *HEX*. Levine's tale, like any effort to summarize a complex intellectual or activist "movement," is necessarily incomplete. Given its focus, it does not address several deeply contentious and publicly known troubles vexing higher education during the period that *HEX* emerged and solidified a perspective on scholarship, the role of higher education in a democracy and the nature of democracy.

Of course a volume such as this will present many opportunities to explore those troubles as has *HEX* itself over the years of its publication. My perspective on the environment in higher education during the *HEX* years differs from Levine's in two ways.

First, I disagree with his implied assertion that the public sphere must privilege open-ended intellectual pluralism. Openness to ideas as described by Levine, suggests to me that more theoretically coherent or ideologically informed perspectives (or some theoretically informed perspectives) are not welcome or are troubling in the public sphere. To that I take issue. I would argue the contrary, which given the scale of problems the public must confront, pragmatic openness is simply inadequate. There are historical moments when *big* abstract theories are required. No, not utopian claims or closed ideologies uncoupled from experience but *big* ideas that require a certain level of intellectual clarity, necessary abstraction, sustained critical analysis, and transparency in terms of how power might give unwarranted credence to some ideas recasting them as common sense, while undermining others as "un-American."

Second, I have a different take on the nature and meaning of the relationship of public work and paid commodified knowledge work. Levine describes *HEX* scholars as engaged in "civic work." His analysis of two generations of such inclined academics focuses primarily on the "civic" dimension of civic work with a nod to the transformations in paid academic labor over the same period. Those transformations appear as backdrop to his story. I argue that they should be center stage. I will argue that civic work, (aka "public work") is the default form of dignified human work inside and outside the academy, as paid labor loses its remaining generative capacity under conditions of neoliberal globalization. Here is where abstract theory of a certain un-American sort is essential.

As presented by Levine, *HEX* authors and civically engaged faculty are rooted in a bedrock commitment to democratic pluralism and deliberative democracy and therefore critical of forms of intellectual analysis that are too totalizing and hence violative of openness. Or, it may seem too abstract and remote from the concrete lives of American citizens.

I argue the contrary. *HEX* authors like all intellectuals, like all people, use implied theories, bits of frameworks, heady ideas, thick concepts as "objects to think with." And, given the changes in theory and practice brought to the table by scholars critical of the liberal tradition (e.g., postcolonial theorists, radical feminists, queer theorists, advocates of poststructuralism and postmodernism), there are a lot more concepts out there. Why bolt from those scholars who frankly offer to work with the public to put the theoretical pieces together in public spaces in public? Not as part of an insider agenda to transform the world but rather as in, "Wow! If you look at things from outside the liberal frame, you might make slightly better sense of your experience and understand what all that lefty stuff going on in Latin America is all about. And maybe why so many throughout the world reflecting on their experience, decide the United States is an imperialist nation."

Given the historical moment we are in and the scale of American action in the world, such fresh perspectives can certainly be useful.

The civic renewal movement is exactly such an effort to help citizens theorize from their experience. *But* it refuses to take on liberalism in its present globalizing form and builds, from my point of view, a blunt wall against some ideas, ignoring them because they are not derived from a presumed American democratic tradition. It does not step outside the lines of the *really big* cognitive frame that Louis Hartz called the "Liberal Tradition in America."

But that liberal tradition is being challenged within the American ivy commonwealth and throughout the world. Hence the froth and angst of the culture wars.

The culture wars are mentioned in Levine's account of *HEX*. And yes, I like his description of how civically engaged authors came to celebrate diversity as a positive good essential to a democracy and the production of knowledge. However, reading his description of diversity, it is not clear what might have catalyzed *HEX* authors to develop such a careful defense of it.

Intense arguments over the canon, about what's in and what's out, were surface manifestations of the slow geological shift in the meaning of knowledge, who controls it and for what purposes over the *HEX*'s years. Such controversies are aspects of any systematic analysis of higher education at present, in the past and surely in the future. They are often not pretty and they are thick with abstractions much as their concrete manifestations—more faces that look like America in more centers of power—may imply activist and prag-matic localized action. In short, someone was talking the talk. New theories about the nature of human experience were essential in prying open public spaces. Introducing new and disruptive ideas just might be a form of praxis. Isn't that one aspect of teaching? Isn't that at least in part, what universities "do"?

My contributions to *HEX* were neither notable for their evenhand-edness and civility nor were they thick narratives of public practice and collaboration. They were in fact designed to be disruptive. Anomalies that they may have been, I think they were important and in rereading them, I think they still are. So I'll revisit my concern with the relation-ships between and among public work, academic work, and paid labor. Levine's piece rolls past the unpleasant and deeply problematic aspects of those relationships. That absence of a critical and theoretically abstract approach to the conundrums of work is, as noted above, my second difference with his analysis of *HEX*. So I will focus on that missing story in his account of *HEX*. That story includes the larger political economy in its contemporary neoliberal globalizing form.

What Is Work Worth Doing? What Does Higher Education Have To Do with This Question?

In Levine's account of two generations in the academy, he lightly wanders into generational motives for entering what used to be quaintly called the "life of the mind." What makes the work of the academy (another quaint term), work worth doing? Why do people put up with macaroni and cheese and student loans even unto Social Security, for a form of work vaguely suspect by a society that may or may not be deeply anti-intellectual? Or in any case, a polity whose gut practicality makes academics seem by definition, woolly headed?

And what does higher education have to do with work in general? Everything of course. Higher education squares many circles. Not just for those who like to read books. It keeps a global and national political economy looking briskly meritorious, fairly dispensing keys to the kingdom of the good life at least at the individual level. For example, O'Toole and Lawler in their 2006 book, *The New American Workplace*, include the modest hope that every worker will become wily and strategic in navigating the new global world of work. Their advice? Educate up. Continually and unendingly. Institutions of higher education (not-for-profit and for-profit alike) will provide those wise workers with just-in-time skills and expertise over a lifetime. No rest for the weary!

There does appear to be a societywide consensus (and "hard" evidence supposedly demonstrating an "education premium") that higher education matters deeply in terms of paid employment. If higher education had nothing to do with paid work and the status that attends some, albeit increasingly fewer jobs, it wouldn't be a site for the energy and angst that appears to consume parents attempting to launch their children and institutions competing for their, ideally high-scoring, tuition-bearing daughters and sons.

The individual tales of woe described by journalist Alexandra Robbins in her 2006 book, *The Overachievers: The Secret Lives of Driven Kids*, is enough to get parents, admissions officers, and kids alike reaching for mighty strong antacids.

Further, higher education is still where many, though certainly not all, of the base blocks of knowledge are quarried. Blocks of knowing that support entire structures of professional practice in every aspect of contemporary existence. Structures that are premised on knowledge "out there" that can be discovered, utilized, taught, packaged, and sold. In short, (using a dollop of Marxist theory here) knowledge that can be alienated from its creators and commodified.

> *"Obviously, one aspect of academic professionalization was, and continues to be, to undermine popular confidence in the 'lay' mind through the creation of professional status and a monopoly of expertise."*
>
> ("Proles, Entrepreneurs, or Public Scholars?," *HEX*, 1998.)

But when David Mathews asked the contributors to this volume to think about how scholarship and professional expertise might be deployed in such a way as to not overwhelm, alienate, or diminish the dignity of citizen "clients," I think we were all reminded that in general the contributors to *HEX* over the years, have spent many, many vexing hours examining their consciences regarding the disabling nature of expertise in a democratic polity regardless of its political economy.

That inquiry included scrutiny of their own expertise as scholars and members of disciplines and professions. How awful that what you might love to do, your own work worth doing, you find complicit in another human being's diminished sense of self? Even more so when you believe that education, at least under present conditions of neoliberal globalization, is the remaining mechanism for upward mobility for those you know did *not* have a childhood spent preparing to show up at the door of an elite institution's admissions office.

This deeply felt and openly expressed examination of conscience regarding the functions and functioning of expertise in a democratic society may be the single most valuable contribution of *HEX* to thinking about higher education.

And so *HEX* authors in their scholarship and practice signal a willful retreat from what expertise and professionalism promised to provide them as scholars. That is, a zone within which they "own" their labor, can hone their competencies and can experience themselves as creative human beings. *HEX* scholars present themselves as willing to share in the name of democracy the very thing—the agency bestowed by expert knowledge that comes with advanced education—that their students are told will ensure them, their students, a work life of creativity and autonomy. And it might be added, take a hatchet to expertise!

What compensates academics, scholars, and professionals for the loss of status and agency that attends the sharing of the expertise, authority, and intellectual privilege that supposedly accompanies a PhD? The story I read in *HEX* is one of steady fleshing out of a new form of work conducted outside the ivied walls and a celebration of the joys that attend that work. Levine terms it *civic work*. It is also termed *public work*.[1]

But when we think of public work in a democracy, we don't usually think "Public Plumber." So why do we assume that there is a Public Scholar, a Public Journalist, a Public Intellectual? This is where the larger dialogue on the external pressures bearing upon higher education comes into play.

Much has been written to date about the work lives of faculty. Foundation-sponsored academic conferences, organizational meetings, and sessions within annual disciplinary meetings have focused on the impact of neoliberal market values on the institutional, disciplinary, and global organizations and contexts within which faculty labor and which constrain and shape the work they do. Books, articles, and think pieces have emerged from those conferences, meetings, and disciplinary sessions.[2]

---

[1] Boyte, "Public Work: An interview with Harry Boyte," and Boyte, *Everyday Politics: Reconnecting Citizens and Public Life.*

[2] Brint, *The Future of the City of Intellect: The Changing American University.*

What seems unavoidable is the conclusion that the middle-class effort to use expertise as a way to sustain privilege and solidify its status, distinguishing its paid work from that of mere "laborers," is under siege. Even among the professoriate. Academics are certifiers but the certified are not immune from the process of capitalist de-skilling. In 1998, I presented in *HEX* a view of faculty and institutions of higher education as challenged and transformed by the not very subtle pressure of market values, incentives, and more ominously, disincentives.[3]

Faculty, I argued, were increasingly positioned to view themselves as entrepreneurs within their various worlds of practice and institutions and hustle accordingly or else. The nightmare alternative; mere worker bee teaching machine, just another weary member of a vast and growing training sector, proletarians in the knowledge factories of postindustrial, globalizing late capitalism. For a powerful fleshing out of my argument, faculty all over the world might wish to reflect upon David Noble's 2002 book *Digital Diploma Mills*. Men and women who prepare and decorate a kingdom of knowledge no longer govern it; are no longer members of an association of producers unless that is, as Noble suggests, they consciously resist those transformations in higher education that seem on first analysis to be inevitable; beyond human or political control. They should do so both for themselves and potentially all workers. But they must first understand the stakes involved in their resistance and maintain a clear-headed appreciation for the tenaciousness of what they're resisting. And it isn't just a "bad apple" dean, harried university president, or shortsighted state legislature.

I'll readily admit that scholars and faculty are not deskilled in the same way that the demand for increased efficiency and productivity press upon the factory worker who having just learned the computer, discovers the robot's taken his job while he was learning CAD at the community college. You can't take away a PhD but you can judge its base of knowledge "old."

---

[3] Stanley, "Proles, Entrepreneurs, or Public Scholars?"

There are many ways to diminish status and discount productive labor, tailored to every job site! As the knowledge-making and disseminating "line" picks up speed, the slackers get identified and, tenured as they may be, they move on down that line, are invited to teach Freshman Intro, nudged from the center of institutional governance and become the "dead weight" that neoliberal assumptions about the atavistic nature of tenure predict. Or, more concretely, do *not* get that merit raise.

For those "gypsy" academics without tenure or for adjuncts, forget dignity, appreciation, health benefits, or time to enjoy either teaching or a social world of work.

For them, moving into the public sphere may well be both a strategic choice but also a way to find work worthy of one's intellectual passions. At least until they discover that the NGO sector and government work have their own pressures and market-based demands bearing upon them.

The dreamy image of the study, the crackling fire, and the classics text opened in the lap while the professor, lost in subtle reverie regarding the perennial foibles of the human condition, sips port is more joke than desired.[4]

Zipping from foundation headquarters to professional meetings to wherever the frontiers of knowledge need a boost or a university a temporary visiting star, "Fast World"[5] entrepreneurial faculty appear more Donald Trump than rumpled tweed no matter the quaintness of the actual costume they wear. Fast World does not encourage wasteful reflection. Unless that is, an organizational expert can "prove" that reflection or a "democratic" workplace or managerial practices that seem superficially democratic (until the pink slip arrives) enhance some aspect of production. Unless reflection creates "value-added," reappears in positive "outcomes," helps achieve a "benchmark," or can be tracked by other profit-driven "assessments," such as the old standby, "the bottom line,"

---

[4] Johnson, et al., *Steal This University: The Rise of the New Imperialism.*

[5] Friedman, *The Lexus and the Olive Tree.*

dump reflection. Perhaps only academic "star power" guarantees time for reflection.

Many discussions of the way faculty and institutions can maintain their "agency" are premised upon the assumption that entrepreneurship variously understood, is the main, if not the only means. Even the titles of recent books on higher education, for example *Remaking the American University: Market-Smart and Mission-Centered*, suggest that market forces must be accommodated, indeed deployed, to salvage the core mission of higher education.[6]

Seldom is the question asked whether entrepreneurship even in its more de-fanged forms and democratic civic life are compatible, although the assumption that they are floats through many discussions of how communities and nations, not just institutions of higher education, can restore their collective agency. But of course, that same institutional and individual agency, hard won as it is through entrepreneurial efforts, is perpetually undermined by globalization in its manifest forms, personally confronted as an unending speed up of work, leisure, family/community life, and even childhood, generated in part by the knowledge producing and disseminating industry itself. Chillingly at least to some, higher education as traditionally understood, may be an increasingly smaller "share" of that industrial sector. Its fixed campuses becoming a metaphoric knowledge industry rust belt as educational virtuality and direct linkage to employment and productivity become the markers of a good education worldwide.[7]

Many who write on institutional change in higher education are quick to add to what otherwise seems their bleak assessment of the future of the professoriate in terms of the nature of the work professors do and the conditions under which they do it, that faculty and institutions of higher education have longstanding cultures and "institutional logics" that work to preserve the heartland. The

---

[6] Zemsky, et al., *Remaking the American University: Market-Smart and Mission-Centered*.

[7] Cox, "None of Your Business: The Rise of the University of Phoenix and For-Profit Education—And Why It Will Fail Us All," 15-32.

heartland is the core of academic life and constituted by those domains (frequently described as the disciplinary homes of faculty or
the liberal arts tradition) of practice still controlled by faculty and
ordered by a lingering commitment to truth through research, increasingly refined methodologies and peer-reviewed scholarship.
"We are a university!" is not an uncommon response to one more
invitation to faculty, colleges, and universities to collaborate with
corporate interests, or other "peripheral" institutions, to commodify
academic labor or produce value-added knowledge products.

Work Worth Doing: *HEX* as a Site for Reimagining the Work of the Mind as Public Work

The contributors to *HEX* are drawn I think to a vision of
democracy that redeems labor of all sorts. It is a vision grounded
in pragmatic, incremental social change within the many civic
workshops of civil society. It suggests that if your paid labor is a
source of angst, you can step into the public sphere or civil society,
engage in public work, and feel yourself stretched to your full
humanity.

But having given up, or set aside, an overt use of left or macroanalysis like Noble's, to illuminate the experiences of actual citizens
working for money under conditions of neoliberalism, *HEX* authors
have fallen back upon a pragmatic, at times anarchistic version of
American liberal democratic exceptionalism and avoid as does
Levine, socialist analysis, or newer theoretical approaches in the
humanities and social sciences. Its anarchistic affinity is revealed
in a public practice that does not easily embrace state power as a
way to balance the increasing power of global economic institutions
(understandable at a time when state power is ballooning in many
spheres in the name of "national security") but rather discovers in
civic associations and civil society fertile ground for civic renewal
and creative collaborative problem solving. Whether "fessing up" to
its debt to Marxism or not, the vision behind the civic renewal movement does reintroduce the ideal of an "association of producers."
Producers who labor not in the neoliberal globalizing marketplace
but work together in civil society. Work worth doing moves from

paid work to public work. From the production of widgets to the coproduction of public goods.[8]

Further, in the name of narrative thickness (all citizens have a story to tell), it avoids the use of concepts that seem initially unrelated to citizens' concrete lives. One person's contemporary hymn to a vital civil society, could be another's updated version of old anarchist dreams. But anarchists told their story in the context of a multiplicity of political theoretical frameworks within and outside liberalism, including socialism. The civic conversation must have been decidedly more edgy in Jane Addam's Hull House!

Deliberative democracy, civic engagement and renewal, and finally your university situated in the commons as against constituting its own separate ivory commonwealth, and you've got a type of work that conceivably supports human dignity and democracy. But I ask whose work? And why the shift from the more traditional meanings of academic work to those that seem to jump on board the democracy train? And is this approach to academic practice and public work sufficient to derail or even slow down that other train? A neoliberal train, which seems to be gathering on board the whole of humanity, forcing its passengers to rush ever faster to a temporal and spatial world that just might destroy our capacity for community, muting our ability to ask whether such a world is generative of a life worth living and if so, for whom?

> *"In the effort to professionalize the mind and certify knowledge, faculty in higher education may have inadvertently undermined the very idea of education as a transcendent public value, a good in itself broadly valued and needed in a democracy."*
>
> ("Proles, Entrepreneurs, or Public Scholars?," *HEX*, 1998.)

---

[8] Sirianni and Friedland, *The Civic Renewal Movement*, 135.

You can hope like the devil that you can reembed the market in civil society and make government a "catalytic" collaborator[9] with citizens but when an angst-ridden business person has to close the plant she may feel the only story she can tell her sister citizens is that, like the weather or the devil, the market made her do it. I say, better to bring on a rich, thick "redistribute" justice frame that does not describe justice as only a struggle over scarce resources but includes a full bore analysis of "culture work," "paid work," and "civic work" supported by rich contemporary strains of theory in the social sciences and humanities, old-fashioned Marxist materialism and the experiences of non-Americans with other ideological and cultural orientations in their heads. No, you do not need to assume false consciousness on the part of anyone. Let's start with a discussion of why people might resist the temporal demands of such a conversation rather than assume they're not interested or can't understand it.

Come on! We had Eugene Debs on the presidential ballot! We can stretch our minds beyond a cramped, cowed liberalism. The civic renewal movement may not be enough to help us do so.

Harry Boyte, a nationally and internationally known scholar-practitioner, and frequent contributor to *HEX*, argues that public work should be premised upon an older tradition of craft.[10] His claim does suggest that the plumber's practice might be a better place to theorize public work than the scholar's. But what is missing in much of Boyte's admirable writings and creative practice presented as a model in the pages of *HEX*, is the overt acknowledgment that capitalism's "job" remains to eliminate the craft tradition by expropriating individually held tools, deskilling out of existence worker competencies and eliminating exactly what the craft tradition once brought many actual workers. Even the plumbers' craft is being rationalized, their work commodified into units of service. Can the craft of public work really compensate for the loss of craft in paid labor? And for whom is this possible? Most citizens confronted

---

[9] Ibid.

[10] Boyte, *Everyday Politics*.

with the necessity of paid work, understand a great deal about how globalization impacts that work. And it is not to encourage craft!

Who then will shape the commons as theorized and practiced by *HEX* scholars? Who will create a public worthy of democratic rhetoric? Frankly who has the time? The contributors to *HEX* and the civic renewal movement it seems. And it would be nice if work in this commons would "count" for tenure and promotion. Even Boyte in his celebration of craft as a model for public work focuses on professionals whom he claims have lost their attachment to the public. He does not focus on plumbers. Of course, he does not mean that they should be excluded from public world making. But he also neglects to note that professionals have hard-won professional expertise as a buffer against the creative destruction of capitalism.

> *"All the shifts, moves, and reallocations of resources large and small, that institutions of higher education do to adapt to and accommodate the power of market institutions are signals and invitations to students to do the same."*
>
> ("The Packaged Self, Modern and Postmodern Persons in Late Capitalist Times: The Challenge to Higher Education," *HEX*, 2000.)

In short, professionals have the possibility of reimagining their labor as public work *because* they have expertise that, at least temporarily, is valued by the public, rewarded by the market, and scampers ahead of the productivity churn that seeks to transform that same expertise into lower paid "homogeneous abstract labor." Professionals have a degree of agency that a service or industrial worker, whose only recourse may be the collective agency of a union, may not. Professional agency rooted in expertise, is nonetheless in the cross hairs of globalization. And many of the young still flocking to institutions of higher education expect that cutting-edge expertise is what they will find within those ivied walls or they will go elsewhere.

A vital, broad (even world-spanning?) liberal civil society with its invitation to professionals to become coproducers of public goods, might signal an acceptance (without question or reflection), that the forces of neoliberalism cannot be stopped. What could function better to support a particular vision of the *good life* defined by liberal capitalism, than a deep acceptance that you are perpetually on the move as a worker and citizen? So get over it! As with paid labor, keep your skill-set fresh, your civic muscles toned. Prepare yourself for civic life by carrying on your back from community to community, job to job, a civic mind-set that can be deployed in any community rather like a paid career that under neoliberal assumptions, demands perpetual spatial and temporal catch-up. And, like the country club for the upper-management family of the 50s, or the PX for those soldiers on the fringes of empire (any time), civil society should be up and running everywhere you go and look a lot like the civil society you just left. Listen:

> If a movement promises to expand partner relationships spatially, so to speak, it also promises to multiply pathways for the development of civic careers over time. A movement that can enlarge our mental maps of kindred forms of democratic work enables citizens to locate opportunities for continued contributions as they move through the life course, change jobs, relocate to different communities, or shift their issue focus and priorities.[11]

Like the paid worker tuned up and ready to pack that U-haul, this broadening civil society will make sure citizens will be less likely to lose their civic identity and "motivation" as a result of "substantial gaps in civic activity."

Time carved out for a rich life embedded in civic associations in one place is less and less available to more and more people, including those in professions whose certification standards keep ramping up. Though people do still try to remain attached to whatever community they parachute into, and *HEX* is filled with examples, the way in which paid labor presses in on family, persons,

---

[11] Sirianni and Friedland, *The Civic Renewal Movement*, 128.

and community life must be, and seldom is, addressed and theorized outside the bottom's up partnershipping among civic associations that is the signature of the civic renewal movement.

Workers and "ordinary" citizens are already aware of the conditions, demands, and contradictions in how paid work is presented and enacted in a late capitalist society. Who doesn't know in their gut that losing a job and then a house and then a community as one wanders looking for a decent job with health benefits and a good 401K plan, cannot be good for the kids?[12] Or, that the pay-off in consumer goods and materialistic values if one finds that job, cannot be good for the souls of the kids either. We know that most paid work is not assigned based upon considered democratic reflection on what is work worth doing or most needed by a society. Is the civic renewal movement really ready to address those experiences? And how long will it take to act on them, given that childhoods all over the world last only so long, or not at all?

Boyte is correct, I think, in trying to mobilize both citizens and faculty to think politically, but his version of relational politics skirts issues central to macropolitical economy and lacks the theoretical scope needed to address them. *But* if we want leaders, including university and college presidents, and citizens to take on the *big* public issues of our times, we must ask them their views on contemporary neoliberalism as experienced not just locally but nationally and internationally as understood through many lenses not all made in America.

Any college or university president can join the local Chamber of Commerce, sit on several citizen committees dedicated to local economic development and discuss how to survive and compete with other cities, regions, states, or communities. But without contributing to and sustaining a deep national conversation on neoliberal globalization, the larger political economy becomes the weather; out there, not of us. Or the "thing" gentlemen and ladies don't discuss.

Students and citizens themselves have focused on big issues and made such framed analysis of them including the worldwide political economy. But student and activist citizens cannot maintain

---

[12] Uchitelle, *The Disposable American: Layoffs and Their Consequences.*

a conversation with the mainstream that explores the credibility of their own ideological claims regarding the political economy unless mainstream institutions support that conversation and their well-meaning elders and leaders are willing to join it for the long haul.

Clearly national security and war have become the *big* issues of our time. Nonetheless the practices and assumptions that support neoliberal globalization as a natural process continue apace and are for the most part, not explored through a critical lens or from theoretical positions outside liberalism. There are many conversations in both the United States and throughout the world about neoliberalism, its linkages to imperialism or in-the-world economic practices that challenge it. Surely university and college presidents can charge their institutions and faculties to go ever deeper into the conundrums, contradictions, and tensions globalization brings to all institutional sectors, including their own. They can invite, even urge, faculty to share their practice, research, and intellectual analysis with the public. They can ask again and again how globalization does or doesn't advance democracy, create the conditions for work worth doing, and provide structural support for human flourishing in the United States and elsewhere, even as they know that their institutional survival may be at risk should they ask too much or do too little to meet market demands.

This may not be such a risk.

There are examples in the world of academic leadership that suggest that a subtle macroconversation is taking place. I do not mean at the insider disciplinary level at which it is hardly subtle. There neoliberalism and globalization are concepts and practices to be embraced or challenged theoretically, methodologically, and with disciplinary focus. I mean at the level of an institution's conversation with the public at all levels—local, national, and international. I am certainly not alone in arguing that such a subtle conversation is being conducted creatively within higher education particularly in the humanities and around diversity.[13] But I want it loud and proud.

---

[13] Veninga and McAfee, *Standing with the Public: The Humanities and Democratic Practice.*

I'll use Syracuse University, where I taught for almost 20 years, as an example of how the culture wars might generate a below the radar critical analysis of neoliberalism in a way that does open up space for *big* ideas. Perhaps my example suffers from the same unwillingness to address macropolitical and economic structures directly. Indeed Syracuse University chancellor Nancy Cantor told me that a critique of neoliberalism is *not* how she frames her practice.

But Chancellor Nancy Cantor has begun a deep critical analysis and conversation with many constituencies over the role of higher education in a democracy. That conversation does acknowledge that higher education is being transformed and shaped by large-scale, macro forces and practices. However, Cantor celebrates that higher education has *also* been transformed by the hard, hard work of intellectual and theoretical analysis, particularly around diversity.

Cantor has signaled at the national level that the world of the academy is not what it once was because of diversity. Not just the diversity of student skin color, sexual orientation, and eye shape, deeply important as those are. But also because of the diversity of intellectual frameworks and theories that have emerged over the last three decades. The two cannot be uncoupled. The thickly theoretical arguments that were used to support the diversity of persons in higher education, have implications for how the human world is and should be ordered, how resources are or should be distributed and power is or should be justified.

They were normative, at times radical, theories but their advocates aspired to intellectual rigor and honesty. Yes, such academics may have become demoralized because their work was often represented to them as gobbledygook, irrelevant to the very society they hoped to challenge and improve (the poor MLA!). A charge raised not just by conservative critics on a screed but even by friends in the academy.

Yes, you can find traces of such contemporary theoretical moves in the perennial great works of the past but you can also find them in the oracular traditions of East Africa and how much the better we are for that! How would we have known how cultural traditions become invisible, marginalized, or degraded without seemingly airy postcolonial theory?

Cantor, I think, meant this far richer view of diversity when she articulated a vision of diversity that helped salvage one mechanism for guaranteeing it, affirmative action. Cantor, as many know, was closely involved in the University of Michigan's defense of affirmative action in the *Grutter* and *Gratz* cases decided by the Supreme Court in 2003.

Universities are spaces for the production of critical nonalienated or alienating ideas. Cantor's practice by celebrating the shops that craft complex, provocative ideas, offers the public a conversation that respects ideas as themselves public goods.

Conclusion

HEX writing is informal, fresh, willing to reveal the situated self of the writer. It's the writing of academics who uncouple themselves from the train of expertise and professionalism, at least for a time. There is no doubt that these same authors can sling the hash with their peers, write for other venues, play or have played the tenure game. But they seem to find in public work something more satisfying, more deeply attuned to what it might mean to do the work of the world than spending their days primarily polishing their expertise. Perhaps, they find work in the commons to be an opportunity to use their poetry, their capacity for humor, their delight in learning something they are not skilled at, their awe at collective world making. As cocreators of the commons, they become crafters and artists, coproducers of public goods that are not easily reduced to commodities.

But if they ignore the necessity of a public and sustained inquiry into why and how our present political economy functions as it does and why and how market values distort not just their own institutions but every institution, our work and your work, they will have settled for bottoms-up, incremental changes.

To keep such a macroanalysis in one's pocket because it might seem too abstract or scholarly, is to enter the commons fearful of the capacity of sister citizens to understand and reflect upon their own experiences. If we enter the commons as citizens, we have to believe that minds can move, especially our own. Education itself is about whether anyone can be taught anything in any manner that freshens the mind and expands the soul as against being a modestly cynical exercise in credentialing. Deep frameworks do change and consciousness of their existence in our own souls, helps change them.

But beyond the assertion that citizens and faculty are complex beings capable of thinking the world anew, there are brute facts as well. Sweet as the *HEX* vision may be, we know that outside those free spaces, factories close, industries move, communities crash, governments fall, power corrupts, war happens, resources are allocated, laws are changed, and people's lives are improved or shattered by those changes.

HEX scholars and practitioners seem to harbor the hope that if they help create a democratic commons, a vital and pluralistic civil society, everyone will come and recognizing each other's humanity beneath the diversity, together begin the long march to recapture many institutional sectors, transforming seemingly rigid structures into polities alive with democracy. If they lose the sense of governance and control in their own institutions of higher education as market pressures and norms reshape those institutions, they can look fondly at civil society hoping that the democratic values nurtured in its cultivation can bleed back into both market and state, transforming them and ultimately higher education as well.

If once in those free spaces, they have to bite their tongue so the plumber can speak, so be it. But maybe the plumber can tell the story that opens up the broader conversation about political economy and the nature of work in our times. Maybe then the scholar will share with the plumber what she knows about the history of labor, about Eugene Debs and Emma Goldman, about the way in which our contemporary world-spanning, neoliberal political economy so vast and seemingly uncontrollable, is a human creation, was once otherwise and could be different. Perhaps the plumber already knows this.

References

Boyte, Harry C. *Everyday Politics: Reconnecting Citizens and Public Life.* Philadelphia: University of Pennsylvania Press, 2004.

Boyte, Harry C. "Public Work: An interview with Harry Boyte." *Higher Education Exchange* (2000): 43-51.

Brint, Steven G. *The Future of the City of Intellect: The Changing American University.* Stanford University Press, 2002.

Collis, D. "New Business Models for Higher Education." In *The Future of the City of Intellect: The Changing American University,* 181-204. Stanford, CA: Stanford University Press, 2002.

Cox, Ana Marie. "None of Your Business: The Rise of the University of Phoenix and For-Profit Education—And Why It Will Fail Us All." In *Steal This University: The Rise of the New Imperialism,* eds. Benjamin Johnson, Patrick Kavanaugh, and Kevin Mattson. New York: Routledge, 2003.

Dickman, H., ed. *The Imperiled Academy.* New Brunswick, NJ: Transaction Publishers, 1993.

Friedman, Thomas. *The Lexus and the Olive Tree.* New York: Anchor Books, 1999.

Friedman, Thomas. *The World Is Flat: A Brief History of the Twenty-first Century,* New York, NY: Farrar, Straus and Giroux, 2006.

Fukuyama, F. *America at the Crossroads: Democracy, Power, and the Neoconservative Legacy.* New Haven, CT: Yale University Press, 2006.

Grandin, G. *Empire's Workshop: Latin America, the United States and the Rise of the New Imperialism.* New York, NY: Metropolitan Books, 2006.

Gumport, P. "The Future of the City of the Intellect," In *The Future of the City of Intellect: The Changing American University,* ed. S. Brint. Stanford, CA: Stanford University Press, 2002.

Johson, Benjamin, Patrick Kavanaugh, and Kevin Mattson. *Steal This University: The Rise of the New Imperialism.* New York: Routledge, 2003.

Lakoff, G. *Whose Freedom? The Battle over America's Most Important Idea.* New York, NY: Farrar, Straus and Giroux, 2006.

Marx, K. *Capital Volume I: A Critique of Political Economy.* London, England: Penguin Books, 1990.

O'Toole J. and Lawler E. *The New American Workplace.* New York, NY: Palgrave MacMillan, 2006.

Peters, Scott, et al., eds. *Engaging Campus and Community: The Practice of Public Scholarship in the State and Land-Grant University System.* Dayton,

OH: Kettering Foundation Press, 2005.

Robbins, A. *The Overachievers: The Secret Lives of Driven Kids.* New York, NY: Hyperion, 2006.

Sirianni, Carmen and Lewis Friedland. *The Civic Renewal Movement: Community-Building and Democracy in the United States.* Dayton, OH: Kettering Foundation Press, 2005.

Stanley, M. "The Packaged Self, Modern and Postmodern Persons in Late Capitalist Times: The Challenge to Higher Education." *Higher Education Exchange* (2000): 28-42.

Stanley, Mary. "Proles, Entrepreneurs, or Public Scholars?" *Higher Education Exchange* (1998): 33-45.

Suissa, J. *Anarchism and Education: A Philosophical Perspective.* London, England: Routledge, 2006.

Tighe, T. *Who's in Charge of America's Research Universities?: A Blueprint for Reform.* Albany, NY: State University of New York Press, 2003.

Uchitelle, Susan. *The Disposable American: Layoffs and Their Consequences.* New York: Knopf, 2006.

Veninga, James and Noëlle McAfee. *Standing with the Public: the Humanities and Democratic Practice.* Dayton, OH: Kettering Foundation Press, 1997.

Zemsky Robert, Gregory R. Wegner, and William F. Massy. *Remaking the American University: Market-Smart and Mission-Centered.* Piscataway, NJ: Rutgers University Press, 2005.

CHAPTER TWO

The Civic Roots of
Higher Education

Should Higher Education
Have a Civic Mission?
Historical Reflections

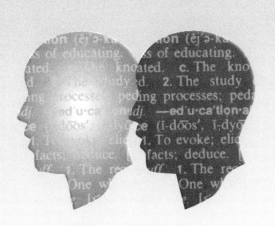

Should Higher Education Have a Civic Mission? Historical Reflections

R. Claire Snyder

What does it mean to say that higher education should have a civic mission? The term *civic* is defined as "of or relating to a citizen, a city, citizenship, or community affairs." The term *citizen* is not just another name for an individual; *citizen* is a membership category that connects the individual to a self-governing community, a city, a republic. The term originated within the democratic tradition of civic republicanism, which dates back to ancient Greece and Rome, to refer not to all who live in a community but specifically to those responsible for public affairs. While contemporary liberal democracy—dedicated to protecting the rights, liberties, and interests of individuals—uses the term *citizen*, it has vacated the category of its historic meaning, responsibility for civic participation. Consequently, the liberal citizen has individual rights but few duties.

To answer the question of whether higher education should have a civic mission requires us to answer the question behind the question: what does citizenship mean? In other words, the theory of democracy people implicitly or explicitly assume directly affects their vision of citizenship and so also shapes their view of higher education's mission. Today liberal democracy with its emphasis on individualism appears to be the dominant vision of democracy in America. But that was not always the case. In the early years of American history, the civic republican vision of democracy played an important role, which is why the United States was founded as a republic. Not reducible to representative government, a republic is a sovereign political community of equal citizens who work together to govern themselves for the common good. Civic republican political theorists ground their belief in popular sovereignty on the Roman principle that "what affects all must be decided by all." Thus, they believe that citizens must actively participate in self-government, if they want to keep their republic.

So to ask whether higher education should have a civic mission in the true sense is to ask whether it should take an active role in preparing students for citizenship, active participation in self-government. Today, many institutions of higher learning no longer have a civic mission in this sense.

> *"It seems to me that all research-scholars could benefit from grappling seriously with the civic import of their own research agendas."*
>
> ("The Civic Roots of Academic Social Science Scholarship in America," *HEX*, 2000.)

While they may serve public purposes by preparing students for participation in society at large, preparation for active civic or political participation is not necessarily a part of higher education. For example, my own university does not have an explicitly stated civic mission, although it strives to "prepare students to address the complex issues facing them in society and to discover meaning in their own lives," as well as to "encourage diversity" and "serve the needs of the student body." If asked whether the university serves civic purposes, the administration would no doubt say that it does: It prepares students to contribute to the world as informed and productive "citizens" (read: individuals), no matter what field of employment they pursue. But this vision does not entail any particular responsibility for participation in the practices of self-government.

While educating students is certainly an important service to society, an increasing number of folks within the academy believe that higher education could do more to instill in students the importance of civic participation in particular, which is needed in order for democracy to work as it should. That is, if democracy requires more than just an arena in which individuals can pursue their own interests and if citizenship involves more than just expressive individualism, then what does higher education need to do? If democratic citizenship involves acting collectively to achieve common goals, then what does higher education need to do to prepare citizens to take on this task?

Democracy and higher education have influenced each other throughout the course of American history. Changes in democratic society affect higher education, as it adapts to meet public needs and demands, while at the same time, higher education shapes democratic society by the way it educates citizens and leaders. In a more republican era, citizens were actively involved in self-government, and higher education played an important role in civic education. Over the course of the 20th century, as America transitioned into a liberal democracy, with an emphasis on individual choice making and fair procedures, higher education came to operate on what William Sullivan calls "a sort of default program of instrumental individualism." In the last decade or so, however, a burgeoning movement that seeks to resuscitate active citizenship has developed within American democracy, and this has been accompanied by parallel movements within higher education aimed at making its mission more traditionally civic. This essay overviews the evolving history of higher education and democratic life in America and argues that higher education needs to revitalize and reconfigure its traditional civic mission in order to prepare students for active participation in self-government.

Religious Publics and Congregational Colleges

Even before the birth of American democracy, institutions of higher education played a central role in public life. The original model of American higher education was the *congregational college*, and throughout the colonial period (and beyond), the congregational college model of higher education served three important public purposes. First, the congregational colleges produced community leaders. Second, they gave those leaders the type of knowledge considered necessary for those responsible for public affairs. Third, the congregational colleges educated future leaders with a curriculum of Christian humanism because they saw normative thinking as central to the process of decision making about public matters.

The Puritan community of the Massachusetts Bay Colony founded Harvard College in 1636 in order to train leaders, those who would govern its Christian commonwealth. The nature of Puritan society directly affected both who its governors would be and what they would study in college. Because the early Puritans wanted a perfectly united community and a public life devoted to serving God, their religious and political spheres were naturally interconnected. Nevertheless, because of Protestant theology and a desire not to replicate the traditional Anglican fusion of church and state, they simultaneously made a conceptual distinction between the two spheres. Thus, while citizenship in the Puritan community required membership in the Congregationalist church, and church leaders took a lead role in political life by sermonizing on Election Day and consulting with civil magistrates, ministers were barred from holding political office and the courts were nonecclesiastical.

Due to the nature of their community, the Puritans needed the leadership of both ministers and lawyers, and so they founded Harvard College to train these men to tend to public affairs. The first institution of Puritan civil society, Harvard developed as a distinct entity, separate from both church and state, yet subject to the authority of both. Although Harvard College trained both sacred and civil leaders, all its students were educated with the same curriculum, a classical (liberal arts) curriculum, which included the great works of moral philosophy, theology, history, and literature. Interestingly, although the study of Scripture took a central place in Puritan education, so did the great pagan works of Plato, Aristotle, and Cicero, among others.

The Puritans considered a classical curriculum that foregrounded normative issues both appropriate and necessary for those who would tend to public affairs—for three reasons. First, the humanistic tradition transmitted to community leaders knowledge of accepted truths as revealed through the great classical and religious texts. Second, studying the liberal arts nurtured in students the inherent political capacity for reflection, a capacity essential to good government. And finally, the classical curriculum was designed to instill in students an excellent moral character.

Like Massachusetts Bay Colony, other homogeneous religious communities also founded colleges to train those who would govern. During the colonial years, a multiplicity of Protestant sects led in turn to a proliferation of church-dominated colleges. The Anglicans founded William and Mary in 1693. The Connecticut Congregationalists founded Yale College in 1701. This pattern of congregationally based colleges accelerated during the first Great Awakening which produced the College of New Jersey (Princeton) founded by the Presbyterians in 1746, Brown founded by the Baptists in 1764, Queen's College (Rutgers) founded by the Dutch Reformed Church in 1766, and Dartmouth founded by the Congregationalists in 1769. In addition, an Old Light coalition with Anglican leadership and Presbyterian support founded King's College (Columbia) in 1754 and the College of Philadelphia (the University of Pennsylvania) in 1755. Despite denominational sponsorship and control, however, these institutions were liberal arts colleges not divinity schools *per se*; they served their particular communities by producing public leaders.

During the 18th century, the character of public life in the colonies began to change. Population growth and colonial sprawl, increased immigration of new European ethnic groups, intermarriage between different sects, and the expansion of commerce, all worked together to create a larger and more heterogeneous public realm—a public realm populated by not only "Yankees," but also the Scotch-Irish, Scots, Germans, and Dutch, not only Congregationalists but also Presbyterians, Quakers, Baptists, Lutherans, Mennonites, Anglicans, members of the Dutch Reformed Church, some Catholics, and a small number of Jews. This burgeoning heterogeneity combined with the flowering of the Enlightenment, as well as monarchical demands for religious freedom and suffrage for Anglicans, created an increasingly tolerant atmosphere in 18th-century America. Moreover, even Puritanism itself began to relax as a second generation, raised under more prosperous conditions and without the hardships of religious persecution, came of age.

Princeton was the first college conceived within the newly formed heterogeneous public. It was the first college chartered in a province with no established church, was the first to receive no state aid and to remain free of state control, and was the first to have intercolonial rather than exclusively local influences. Although deeply influenced by its Presbyterian founders, Princeton was hospitable to students from a variety of sects. As American public life was becoming more diverse, institutions like Princeton emerged to accommodate these changes.

The American Republic and the Emergence of the People's Colleges

As the American Revolution approached, the colonial colleges continued to offer a classical liberal arts curriculum foregrounding normative issues—but with some important modifications. First, higher education began placing a greater emphasis on teaching students to exercise their own personal judgment rather than just absorbing the great truths—a pedagogical method more appropriate for a self-governing republic. Second, as the American public became more concerned about questions of political legitimacy, the colonial colleges followed suit by beginning to allow discussions of overtly political topics. Third, colleges continued to train community leaders for civil society, but these leaders less often filled the pulpits and more often did the practical work of planning the revolution. And finally, the trend toward greater attention to politics accelerated with the addition of political philosophy to the standard curriculum. One might say that the liberal arts were becoming the civic arts.

American political ideals during the 18th century were becoming less religious and more republican, and many colleges followed this trend. The Enlightenment's emphasis on universal reason undergirded international struggles for popular sovereignty and republican self-government rather than clerical or monarchical rule. Out of this Enlightenment context came the American Revolution and the constitutional establishment of a civic republic, instead of a Christian commonwealth. This revolutionary approach to government raised the question of how morality would be upheld without an official church. Thomas Jefferson, following the democratic republican theorist Jean-Jacques Rousseau, believed that a civic republic must provide citizens with a common set of moral values to replace traditional religion and that colleges and universities should play a key role in disseminating this new civil religion. Jefferson wanted the secular government to organize a common educational system, including public universities. Republican government as the instrument of the public should support non-religious institutions of higher education with the civic mission of educating both citizens and public leaders, all of whom would play a role in the self-governing republic.

The changes inaugurated by the American Revolution led to the creation of a new model of higher education more appropriate for the new democratic republic: the *people's college*. Examples include Thomas Jefferson's secular University of Virginia, women's colleges, land-grant universities, and historically black colleges. Because the people's colleges prepared students for participation in self-government, their public purposes constitute a civic mission, in the full sense. The civic mission of the people's colleges continued to include the three public purposes traditionally embraced by the congregational colleges—the production of public leaders, the dissemination of important knowledge, and the development of the type of normative, reflective thinking considered necessary for good public decision making—however, they also added to the traditional list. First, the people's colleges increased public access to higher education beyond an elite group of men, thus beginning to democratize it. Second, rather than simply nurturing the reflective capacities of students, the people's colleges pioneered the idea of applying knowledge to practical public problems, connecting higher education to the collective work necessary to produce a commonwealth or republic, which Harry Boyte has termed *public work*.

In 1819, Jefferson succeeded in founding the University of Virginia, a state-sponsored university that did not have an official religious affiliation. To fend off accusations of godlessness, Jefferson invited particular denominations to set up divinity schools nearby, so that students could get whichever sectarian viewpoint they chose, while also receiving the benefits of a heterogeneous, civic university. (The denominations did not take him up on his offer.) Nevertheless, while the University of Virginia represents a new model of higher education, it was also an anomaly; the vast majority of colleges continued to be denominationally founded and controlled.

> *"Ironically, women's exclusion from electoral politics helped transform them into active citizens."*
>
> ("Women, Social Science, and Public Work During the Progressive Era," *HEX*, 2005.)

With the exception of U.Va., during the early 19th century, congregational colleges that were very closely linked to particular communities rapidly proliferated. Between 1800 and 1861, the number of colleges increased tenfold—and that is only counting those that actually survived. Communities wanted their sons to be educated locally, and having a local college became a key component of civic pride. On the whole, however, because particular communities tended to be religiously homogeneous, the rapid expansion of locally rooted colleges also reinforced their denominational character. Although many of these "colleges" were actually more like glorified high schools, the point remains that in the early 19th century, communities saw institutions of higher education as central to civic life.

During the early republican period of American history, women's education gained importance. The ideal of "republican motherhood" —that women have a special civic role to play in educating future citizens—bolstered the cause of women's education. In 1792, Sarah Pierce founded the first women's college, the Litchfield Female Academy in Connecticut, which existed until 1833. That same year, Oberlin College was founded by liberal Congregationalists as the first coeducational institution in the country, and by 1835 it was racially inclusive as well. A number of women's colleges were founded during the 19th century, including George Female College (Wesleyan) in 1839, Saint Mary-of-the-Woods College in 1840, Mills College in 1852, Vassar in 1861, Hunter College in 1870, Smith in 1871, Wellesley in 1875, Spelman, the first college for African American women, in 1881, Bryn Mawr and Mount Holyoke in 1888, and Barnard in 1889.

The Morrill Act of 1862 and the resulting land-grant movement broadened the civic purposes of higher education in three major ways. First, the land-grant colleges were founded to serve the "agricultural and industrial masses"—90 percent of the American population at that time—and so greatly democratized access to higher education. Second, these institutions combined the liberal arts curriculum with an agricultural and mechanical education, which would enable students to return to their local communities and engage in the "public work" of community problem solving. Third, as Scott Peters has argued, the land-grant colleges pioneered the idea of the "socially-engaged university," a direct contrast with the German-inspired model of detached universities that would come to dominate during the 20th century. These colleges continued the tradition of training those who would govern public affairs, but who those people were, what they studied, and how they applied that knowledge, expanded in accordance with public needs.

During this same time period also came the first historically black colleges which sought to bring the traditional benefits of higher education to black communities. While the first black college was founded by a Quaker in 1837, most were established after the Civil War. Founded by white philanthropists in conjunction with black churches, these new private colleges, like the land-grant institutions, combined a traditional liberal arts curriculum aimed at nurturing the capacity for reflection and creating a strong moral character with the practical skills and knowledge necessary for black community problem solving. These colleges strove to train the leadership necessary for black community autonomy, in this case primarily teachers. Of course, given the circumstances most of these "colleges" were actually more like secondary schools—as was the case with many white religious schools, as noted above. Nevertheless, the important point here is that black communities saw these colleges as central to citizenship.

Liberal Democracy and the Modernist Research University

The third model of American higher education, which William Talcott calls the *modernist research university*, departs markedly from both the congregational college and the people's college. Directly influenced by the German ideal of the detached university, this new model developed in the context of many watershed changes in the nature of American public life and significantly altered the face of higher education in America. While these modernist research universities continued to produce public leaders, these leaders would come to be understood primarily as experts and professionals, rather than moral leaders or active citizens. While the modernist research universities continued to provide future leaders with important knowledge, the curriculum began to foreground the ostensibly impartial natural and social sciences, rather than the explicitly normative approaches of religion and the humanities. And finally, while the modernist research universities continued to teach the type of thinking necessary for public decision making, an emphasis on scientific objectivity and professional expertise began to eclipse the traditional focus on philosophical reflection and deliberation. The modernist research universities were part of the modernist response to modernization.

The emergence of the modernist research university relates directly to changes in American public life. In the latter part of the 19th century, the abolition of slavery, the emergence of modern economic classes, an increasingly diverse new immigrant population, and the growth of cities, all resulted in a much more heterogeneous and conflictual American public, and fear of this increasing diversity led to a variety of attacks on popular sovereignty, including the Progressive emphasis on professional governance through the use of social science as a way of transcending politics. At the same time, the unfolding of industrialization and the expansion of the American market created the need for a modern state to regulate industry and commerce and for professionals to staff the new bureaucracies. In the end, the great Progressive dream of harnessing the new professions and social sciences for the common good ultimately ushered in the "professional politics paradigm"—the idea that the public must be governed by experts and professionals.

The idea of professional politics fits much better with a liberal model of democracy than it does with the more participatory tradition of civic republicanism. Indeed, the republican tradition includes a deep suspicion of professional elites. For example, during the American founding, the republican antifederalists insisted that many people should take turns serving as representatives because they feared the creation of an aristocracy, which could undermine the fragile new republic. And like their republican forebears, they vehemently opposed the creation of a professional military, preferring militias comprised of citizen-soldiers. A republic requires an active citizenry.

In contrast to this, the liberal model of democracy emphasizes individual interests rather than active citizenship. While some individuals may choose to pursue an active political life, many prefer to spend their time on other things, like business matters, for example. Indeed, specialization and the division of labor are hallmarks of economic liberalism, which developed alongside political liberalism. Liberal democracy does not emphasize an engaged citizenry and has no problem delegating governmental duties to professional politicians, as long as they are ultimately accountable to the people. In fact, Talcott emphasizes the connection of the modernist research universities to the procedural model of liberal democracy, which came to dominate American politics during the early 20th century.

The modernist research university emerged concurrently with the professional politics paradigm. As we have seen, prior to the creation of the modernist university, higher education focused on conveying a finite body of knowledge that came out of the classical humanistic tradition. The goal was to nurture the reflective capacities of students and to instill in them an excellence of character. However, with the development of science came the idea that professors could actually produce new knowledge, an approach undergirded by the German university model that was developing around the same time. Consequently, professors began specializing in particular areas in which they would generate original scholarship and eventually become experts.

Many, like the members of the American Social Science Association, hoped that the new field of social science could be used for social reform, that it could provide objective solutions to the myriad of new social problems and political conflicts plaguing American society. However, the early concern with using knowledge for social reform soon came to conflict with the ideal of objectivity, and the originally unified approach to social science fragmented into specialized academic disciplines (e.g., economics, sociology, political science), each of which claimed authority over a particular segment of reality.

By 1915, the increasingly influential modernist universities had, for the most part, broken with the traditional normative concerns of higher education. This break marks a shift from a philosophical and values-based approach to public life to a scientific and professional one, and it must be understood as a part of a general epistemological shift from religion to science that was going on in America during these same years. It also illustrates a transition from the republican ideals of an engaged citizenry, the common good, and collective action to the liberal vision of individualism, private interests, and specialization.

With the ascendancy of the modernist research university, the civic mission of American higher education began to change. The invention of public opinion polls, the psychoanalytic discovery of the unconscious, mass support for communism and fascism, and the increasing relativism within the academy, all led professional elites to question the valorization of popular participation in politics. Some even proclaimed the public "irrational." What's more, an emerging suspicion of "indoctrination"—a reaction to totalitarianism—made universities reluctant to teach any values in any substantive way, even civic ones, and reinforced the need for scientific objectivity.

The Paradox of the Community Colleges

Ironically, the community college movement arose out of the desire of elite universities to protect themselves from "the masses." In the words of James Russell, dean of the Columbia Teachers' College, "If the chief objective of government be to promote civil order and social stability, how can we justify our practice in schooling the masses in precisely the same manner as we do those who are to be our leaders?" In order to protect university research and professional training programs from the onslaught of the supposedly ignorant public and to prevent the creation of an overly educated workforce, administrators at elite institutions like Columbia and the University of Chicago proposed the creation of two-year colleges offering the public vocational training. While these "junior" colleges would offer a college-prep option, two-thirds to three-quarters of junior college students were expected to track into terminal vocational programs.

Interestingly, citizens did not want vocational education; they wanted a traditional liberal arts education, and so people refused to enroll in the vocational tract. In fact, until the 1970s, only 25 to 30 percent of students ever opted for vocational training. Junior colleges appealed to the public only as stepping stones toward traditional four-year institutions. Consequently, out of an elitist attempt to insulate higher education from the public came the proliferation of two-year liberal arts colleges—the birth of the community college move-

> *"The ideal of objectivity increasingly eclipsed the civic value of public engagement on which the American Social Science movement was built. In short, academic social science scholarship lost sight of its original civic purposes."*
>
> ("The Civic Roots of Academic Social Science Scholarship in America," *HEX*, 2000.)

ment, a version of the people's college. And in the tradition of the land-grant institutions, these new community colleges sought to expand access to higher education, nurture the capacity for reflection through a traditional liberal arts curriculum, and prepare students to engage in public work—this time in cities as well as in small communities.

Democratization during the Cold War

Changes in American politics and public life that occurred after World War II directly affected the evolution of the modernist research university. It was during this period that liberal individualism became the dominant principle of American democracy, as the country engaged in the cold war against Communist collectivism. Higher education began a period of major democratization, in the sense of becoming accessible to more and more citizens, beginning with the Truman Report (1947) and the subsequent GI Bill. In 1958, the National Defense Education Act proclaimed that "the security of the Nation requires the fullest development of mental resources and technical skills of its young men and women." This act further expanded federal programs of institutional and individual financial aid. With massive federal assistance, the number of two- and four-year institutions of higher education multiplied. In addition, racial and religious barriers to admission were officially ended.

While the academy's massive postwar expansion did in fact lead to the largest democratization of higher education in the history of the world, this expansion was justified by the cold war idea that we could undermine potential support for communism among working people by providing individuals with the opportunity to achieve personal prosperity. Consequently, cold war universities began to pioneer the idea that higher education should serve the public by advancing the career goals of individual students, rather than by preparing them for civic participation *per se*. This change corresponded with the accelerating shift towards liberal individualism and what Michael Sandel calls the "procedural republic," which simply leaves individuals free to pursue their own interests.

Second, cold war universities continued to focus on the practical application of higher learning, but the focus tipped towards serving economic and military needs, rather than preparing citizens to engage in "public work." In any event, American higher education continued preparing experts and professionals for leadership positions, but, as William Sullivan notes, they increasingly educated them using a "default curriculum" that stressed instrumental individualism, positivism, and the fact/value distinction, rather than maintaining the traditional emphasis on citizenship, civic values, and philosophical reflection.

Thus, despite the greatest democratization of higher education ever realized, American higher education became further disconnected from its traditional civic mission. While a college education was becoming widely available to members of the American public, the content of that education had shifted. The curriculum began to focus less and less on nurturing civic capacities and more and more on serving the professional and vocational interests of individual students. So while colleges and universities increasingly focused on producing experts and professionals, they deemphasized the historical goal of educating citizens to participate in democratic self-government.

The reductionist push to turn colleges and universities into credentialing services for individual students moved higher education away from its traditional civic mission, yet the dominant "economic model" did not end higher education's long civic history. Instead, a movement has developed within higher education that seeks to revitalize and reconfigure its traditional civic mission. This new trend began to develop during the 1960s. For example, the (white) student movement focused much of its attention on democratizing higher education in terms of access, content, and control. That is, in 1961 Students for a Democratic Society (SDS), an organization that wanted American democracy to become more participatory, criticized universities for their lack of civic mission and their service to the military-industrial complex. Bemoaning the apathy of most college students, SDS argued that the mind-set of their peers was produced in part by the type of education they received at college: "Apathy is not simply an attitude; it is a product of social institutions, and of the structure and organization of higher education itself." They specifically criticized the academy's overemphasis on objectivity and specialization and pointed out the ways the university reflects the norms of the larger society, even as it helps shape them.

In addition, the civil rights movement, including the black student movement, also sought the democratization of higher education. In 1962, James Meredith became the first African American student to enroll in the University of Mississippi, protected by federal marshals. In 1963, despite the efforts of George Wallace, Vivian Malone and James Hood registered for classes at the University of

Alabama. The Civil Rights Act of 1964 prohibited state colleges and universities from discriminating on the basis of race. The creation of black studies programs in the late 1960s (and women's studies in the 1970s) extended the academy's commitment to democratizing higher education.

Yet while allowing all citizens access to higher education and including their concerns in college and university curricula should have a central place in any truly civic vision of higher education, democratizing admissions does not necessarily move higher education beyond liberal individualist notions of citizenship and reconnect it to a civic (republican) mission. Consequently, many of the concerns expressed during the 1960s continued to fester and fed into the creation of service-learning programs 20 years later. During the mid-1980s, many educators were becoming increasingly concerned about the media portrayal of college students as materialistic, self-absorbed, and uninterested in helping their neighbors. In response, the presidents of Georgetown, Brown, and Stanford founded Campus Compact in 1985. They believed, however, that public perceptions of college students were false. Many students at their institutions were involved in community service, and the presidents believed many more would follow suit if given the proper encouragement and supportive structures.

After the Cold War: Toward a New Civic University?

With the end of the cold war, American higher education faced a new opportunity to reconfigure its role in public life. As Bill Richardson put it in 1996:

> Higher education played a major role—albeit a discreet one—in winning the Cold War…. Well, we've won the war…. [Therefore,] one of the critical challenges for higher education is to redirect our knowledge and our resources in the service of rural communities and urban neighborhoods. In fact, it may be these investments that prove the true test and value of our research and outreach programs. Can we, for example, make a difference in the lives of people where they live? Can we build the capacity of people to play a central role in

finding their own solutions? And, can we impact public policy that creates both economic and social opportunities for people to improve the quality of life?

Responding to this challenge, a colloquium of university and college presidents issued a "Declaration on the Civic Responsibility of Higher Education" (1999). This document calls for the creation of a "national movement to reinvigorate the public purposes and civic mission of higher education," so that our colleges and universities will once again become "vital agents and architects of a flourishing democracy." This declaration built directly on the very similar "Wingspread Declaration on the Civic Responsibilities of Research Universities," which was issued the previous month by Campus Compact, the American Council on Education, and a wide variety of other organizations and individuals.

Since its founding, Campus Compact has developed into a "national coalition of more than 950 college and university presidents—representing some 5 million students—dedicated to promoting community service, civic engagement, and service-learning in higher education." Subsequently, in 2004 the American Association of State Colleges and Universities started the "American Democracy Project," focusing on institutions not affiliated with Campus Compact. This project is "a multi-campus initiative that seeks to create an intellectual and experiential understanding of civic engagement for undergraduates" at member institutions and "produce graduates who understand and are committed to engaging in meaningful actions as citizens in a democracy."

The burgeoning movement towards resuscitating and reconfiguring the civic mission of higher education relates to a number of changes in public life. First, during the last decades of the 20th century, politics became a battlefield. The so-called "consensus" of the 1950s broke apart during the 1960s, as the nation found itself torn over questions of race and gender, war and peace, sexual liberation and traditional morality. The politics of divisiveness gained steam during the 1970s, when evangelical Christians entered politics en masse in opposition to many of the changes spearheaded by new social movements of the 1960s, including the Equal Rights

Amendment, lesbian/gay rights, abortion, and religious issues, among other things.

> *"My hope is that through historically informed public reflection on the proper relationship between the public and its colleges, we might be able to hasten a reconnection of higher education to public life. Then perhaps colleges and universities can once again meet public needs, this time through facilitating the hard work of public-building and by fostering the practices of deliberative democracy."*
>
> ("The Public and Its Colleges: Reflections on the History of American Higher Education," *HEX*, 1998.)

The resulting "culture wars" accelerated with the end of the cold war, when conservatives and others gained greater political space to turn their attention more fully toward perceived problems inherent in American culture. In 1992, Pat Buchanan declared, "There is a religious war going on in our country for the soul of America. It is a cultural war, as critical to the kind of nation we will one day be as was the Cold War itself." Media coverage of the culture wars portrayed the public as hopelessly divided into two warring camps, and this highlighted the need for people to come together and find common ground.

Second, partially in response to the culture wars that threatened to pull America apart, many citizens began calling for a more deliberative approach to political and social conflict. For example, in 1981 National Issues Forums (NIF)—first called the Domestic Policy Association—was founded to foster deliberation and give citizens a larger role in setting the normative direction for public policy. Over the past 25 years, NIF, "a network of civic, educational, and other organizations, and individuals, whose common interest is to promote public deliberation in America,... has grown to include thousands of civic clubs, religious organizations, libraries, schools, and many other groups that meet to discuss critical public issues."

Finally, the already burgeoning civic movement gained momentum, as studies revealing low levels of political and civic engagement began to concern a lot of people, particularly educators. For example, in the 1996 presidential election, less than half of voting-age Americans went to the polls (49 percent), reportedly the lowest turnout since 1924. Congressional races fared even worse; the self-proclaimed "Republican revolution" of 1994 was authorized by only 38 percent of eligible voters. Worst of all, vitally important presidential primaries have attracted as few as 5 percent of voting-age Americans.

In addition, political participation beyond voting has declined. Robert Putnam argued in "Bowling Alone" (1995):

> Since 1973 the number of Americans who report that "in the past year" they have "attended a public meeting on town or school affairs" has fallen by more than a third (from 22 percent in 1973 to 13 percent in 1993). Similar (or even greater) relative declines are evident in responses to questions about attending a political rally or speech, serving on a committee of some local organization, and working for a political party. By almost every measure, Americans' direct engagement in politics and government has fallen steadily and sharply over the last generation, despite the fact that average levels of education—the best individual-level predictor of political participation—have risen sharply throughout this period. Every year over the last decade or two, millions more have withdrawn from the affairs of their communities.

In addition, while relatively stable for the last 50 years, "political knowledge levels are, in many instances, depressingly low," particularly among "women, African Americans, the poor and the young," as Michael Delli Carpini and Scott Keeter explain in *What Americans Know About Politics and Why It Matters* (1996). Moreover, "as the amount of detail requested increases and as less visible institutions or processes are asked about, the percentage of the public able to correctly answer questions declines." Newspaper reading has declined markedly, especially among the young. Stephen and Linda Bennett find that while in 1966 sixty percent of first-year college students thought "keeping up to date with political affairs" was "essential" or "very important," in 2000 only twenty-eight percent thought so —"the lowest percentage" since the freshman-year survey began and particularly striking in a presidential election year.

In response to these changes in public life, "democratic theory" developed as an academic field within higher education that explicitly seeks to strengthen American democracy. While Benjamin R. Barber's *Strong Democracy* (1984), Robert Bellah's *Habits of the Heart: Individualism and Commitment in American Life* (1985), and Jürgen Habermas' *The Transformation of the Public Sphere* (trans. 1989) constitute foundational works in the field, it wasn't until the 1990s that democratic theory really took off. During that decade, Amatai Etzioni was pivotal in developing and popularizing communitarianism, which seeks to empower communities and revitalize public life. Michael Sandel popularized the communitarian critique of liberalism with his book *Democracy's Discontent* (1996). That same year, Amy Gutmann and Dennis Thompson published *Democracy and Disagreement*, making the case for public deliberation. Many other authors also played an important role in developing the academic field of democratic theory. These academic ideas both shaped and mirrored changes in the public sphere and gave intellectual support to efforts to revitalize higher education's civic mission.

A Fork in the Road

Today we are in a period of tremendous flux, and we face the proverbial fork in the road. Will American democracy continue down the path of liberal individualism and partisan conflict, even if that means important public problems that require collective action will remain unaddressed? Or will we move in a more participatory and deliberative direction? While higher education in many ways mirrors the larger society, it also plays a role in shaping society as well. If people want a more civically engaged democracy that does a better job of addressing public problems, higher education should once again explicitly embrace a strong civic mission and play its historic role in helping democracy work as it should.

References

Banks, William M. *Black Intellectuals: Race and Responsibility in American Life*. New York: W.W. Norton, 1996.

Bennett, Stephen Earl and Linda M. Bennett. "What Political Scientists Should Know about the Survey of First-Year Students in 2000." *PS: Political Science and Politics* 34 (2001): 295-299.

Boyte, Harry and Elizabeth Hollander (on behalf of participants at Wingspread conference). "Wingspread Declaration on the Civic Responsibilities of Research Universities." http://www.compact.org/initiatives/research_universities-wingspread_declaration (accessed August 8, 2007).

Boyte, Harry C. and Nancy N. Kari. "Renewing the Democratic Spirit in American Colleges and Universities: Higher Education as Public Work." In *Higher Education and Civic Responsibility*, edited by Tom Ehrlich. New York: National Council on Education/Oryx Press series, 2000.

Brint, Steven and Jerome Karabel. *The Diverted Dream: Community Colleges and the Promise of Educational Opportunity in America, 1900-1985*. New York: Oxford University Press, 1989.

Carnegie Foundation for the Advancement of Teaching and the Center for Information and Research on Civic Learning and Engagement. "Higher Education: Civic Mission and Civic Effects." http://www.civicyouth.org/PopUps/higher_ed_civic_mission_and_civic_effects.pdf (accessed May 19, 2006).

Delli Carpini, Michael X. and Scott Keeter. *What Americans Know About Politics and Why It Matters*. New Haven, CT: Yale University Press, 1996.

Diamond, Sara. *Roads to Dominion: Right-Wing Movements and Political Power in the United States*. New York: Guilford Publications, 1995.

Ehrlich, Thomas and Elizabeth Hollander (for the Presidents' Leadership Colloquium.) "Presidents Fourth of July Declaration on the Civic Responsibility of Higher Education." http://www.compact.org/resources/declaration.assessment (accessed August 8, 2007).

Evans, Sara M. *Born for Liberty: A History of Women in America*. New York: Free Press Paperbacks, 1997.

Gutmann, Amy and Dennis Thompson. *Democracy and Disagreement*. Cambridge, MA: The Belknap Press of Harvard University Press, 1996.

Hill, Susan T. "The Traditionally Black Institutions of Higher Education: 1860-1982." Washington, DC: The Superintendent of Documents, US Government Printing Office, 1985.

Hofstadter, Richard and Walter P. Metzger. *The Development of Academic Freedom in the United States.* New York and London: Columbia University Press, 1955.

Marsden, George M. *The Soul of the American University: From Protestant Establishment to Established Non-Belief.* New York: Oxford University Press, 1994.

Peters, Scott. "Extension Work as Public Work: Reconsidering Cooperative Extension's Civic Mission." PhD diss. The University of Minnesota, 1997.

Putnam, Robert. "Bowling Alone: America's Declining Social Capital. *Journal of Democracy.* http://xroads.virginia.edu/~hyper/DETOC/assoc/bowling.html (accessed December 18, 2006).

Ricci, David. *The Tragedy of Political Science: Politics, Scholarship, and Democracy.* New Haven and London: Yale University Press, 1984.

Richardson, William C. "Coming in from the Cold War: A Peacetime Mission for Higher Education." Address given to the National Association of State Universities and Land-Grant Colleges, Kellogg Commission News Conference, Washington, DC, January 30, 1996.

Sandel, Michael. *Democracy's Discontent: America in Search of a Public Philosophy.* Cambridge, MA: The Belknap Press of Harvard University Press, 1996.

Snyder, R. Claire. "Should Political Science Have a Civic Mission? An Overview of the Historical Evidence," *PS: Political Science and Politics* XXXIV, no. 2 (2001): 301-305.

Snyder, R. Claire. "The Civic Roots of Academic Social Science Scholarship in America," *Higher Education Exchange* (2000): 5-16.

Snyder, R. Claire. "Shutting the Public Out of Politics: Civic Republicanism, Professional Politics, and the Eclipse of Civil Society." Occasional paper. Dayton, OH: The Kettering Foundation, 1999.

Students for a Democratic Society. "Port Huron Statement." http://coursesa.matrix.msu.edu/~hst306/documents/huron.html (accessed October 27, 2006).

Sullivan, William M. "The University as Citizen: Institutional Identity and Social Responsibility." Washington, DC: The Council on Public Policy Education, 1999.

Talcott, William. "Modern Universities, Absent Citizenship? Historical Perspectives." CIRCLE Working Paper 39. http://www.civicyouth.org/PopUps/Working Papers/WP39Talcott.pdf (accessed December 18, 2006).

Titlebaum, Peter, Gabrielle Williamson, Corinne Daprano, Janine Baer, and Jayne Brahler. "Annotated History of Service-Learning: 1862-2002." http:// servicelearning.org/welcome_to_service-learning/ history/index. php?search_term=history (accessed August 8, 2007).

Tolchin, Susan. *The Angry American: How Voter Rage Is Changing the Nation.* 2nd edition. Boulder, CO and Oxford: Westview Press, 1999.

CHAPTER THREE

Public Work:
The Perspective
and a Story

Public Work: Civic Populism
versus Technocracy in
Higher Education

Public Work at Colgate:
An Interview with
Adam Weinberg

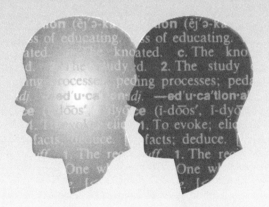

Public Work: Civic Populism versus Technocracy in Higher Education

Harry C. Boyte

Public work as democratic citizenship involves the sustained, visible efforts of a diverse mix of people who create things (material or cultural) of lasting civic significance, whose value is determined by public conversation. Understood in these terms, public work expands concepts of the citizen, democracy, and the engaged institution. It also suggests a strategic reconfiguration of social, cultural, and political energies. Higher education has a critical role to play.

Public work posits the citizen as the responsible and foundational agent of democracy—democracy's cocreator, not simply a voter, volunteer, customer, or protestor who demands his or her fair share of the goods. Democracy is not mainly elections, laws, and institutions but a society, a lived cultural experience, "not just out there in the public sphere," as Barbara Cruikshank has put it, "but in here, at the very soul of subjectivity." Government is best conceived not as prime mover but as catalyst and resource of citizens, neither the problem nor the solution. Democracy is, in fact, a kind of work. Its labors occur in multiple sites, enlist multiple talents in addressing public problems, and result in multiple forms of common wealth. The public works of democracy create an environment of equal respect.

Higher education takes on many roles in such a democracy. Our institutions are its "agents and architects," as Elizabeth Hollander and I put it in *The Wingspread Declaration* on the civic mission of research universities. They are not simply its researchers, critics, service providers, or the educators of its future leaders. Scholars, in turn, are engaged public figures, part of the world. Their work is not only to analyze and critique but also to stimulate conversations, to expand the sense of the possible, and to activate broader civic and political energies.

> *"There are immense obstacles to democracy being taken seriously . . . in higher education. . . . The trend has been toward career preparation, specialized knowledge based on the model of science, and what might be called expert system-maintenance. This has a 'public service' aspect, but it is technocratic."*
>
> ("Public Work: An interview with Harry Boyte," *HEX*, 2000.)

Redefining higher education's role in these terms is crucial in the early 21st century. Higher education is the premier knowledge institution in an era of exploding knowledge and knowledge technologies. It creates knowledge and it also credentials knowledge. It generates and diffuses conceptual frameworks that structure practices of all sorts, from global finance to parent education. It trains and socializes professionals.

Higher education is thus a theater for action of high strategic significance if it takes up a robust democracy-building mission and identity. As Ira Harkavy and Nick Longo have observed, there are rich traditions to draw upon. William Raney Harper, for instance, first president of the University of Chicago, envisioned universities as prophets of democracy. "The university, I maintain, is the prophetic interpreter of democracy," he declared. "[It is] the prophet of her past, in all its vicissitudes; the prophet of her present, in all its complexity; the prophet of her future, in all its possibilities."

If our institutions become infused with a renewed sense of democratic prophetic purpose, they will also help build flourishing democratic societies. The chief obstacle, in my view, is an opposing technocratic politics rooted in higher education. Technocratic politics —domination by experts removed from a common civic life—has spread throughout contemporary society like a silent disease. It is largely a politics without a name, presenting itself as an objective set of truths, practices, and procedures. Technocratic politics turns groups of people into abstract categories. It decontextualizes "problems" from the civic life of communities. It privatizes the world and creates cultures based on a philosophy of scarcity. It profoundly erodes the subjective experience of equal respect.

Public work counters the impersonal, abstract, decontextualized culture of technocracy and its associated left versus right politics. At the molecular level of everyday experience, public work brings back a view of politics as about negotiating the plural, grounded, sometimes conflicted but also relational qualities of the human condition in order to solve problems. At a somewhat larger level of analysis it recasts professional work as a public craft, with experts "on tap, not on top," to use the organizing phrase. At the largest level of analysis, public work is an important ingredient in a strategic reconceptualization that emphasizes movement-building alliances to advance democratic society. Such movement building reaches far beyond elections, ideologies, and formal institutions of government to advance democratic values like equality, openness, participation, respect, and the commonwealth in many arenas, in a time when such values face enormous threat.

The features of this approach, what might be called civic populism, have rich antecedents, but to draw on them effectively requires a sharp strategic shift in emphasis. Although the reference point for today's politics continues to be the cultural and political wars of the 1960s, the more relevant period to look at for direction is the 1930s.

Technocratic Politics

Technocracy—control over significant portions of life by detached, formally credentialed experts—is a pattern and philosophy of governance with particular force in a knowledge society. The characterization of our country as a knowledge society grows from the work of theorists like Raymond Aron and Daniel Bell a generation and more ago. Bell and others drew attention to the increasing role of knowledge creation as a source of power in its own right. Energy generated by steam and electricity transformed preindustrial societies into industrial societies. Money replaced raw materials as the main strategic resource. Today, data-transmission systems and the theoretical knowledge required to organize information are the driving forces of innovation, strategic resources and power, shaping a world economy, changing the pattern of human relationships. "The industrial era was characterized by the influence of humankind over things, including Nature as well as the artifacts of Man," wrote Harlan Cleveland, an astute analyst of knowledge-as-a-resource. "The information era features a sudden increase in humanity's power to think, and therefore to organize." Such a process, in turn, puts those who do the conceptual organizing in a particularly powerful position. One does not have to subscribe to the most extravagant claims that we are entering a qualitatively new world, or that the forms of organization, social, and class structure associated with capitalist society are rapidly dissolving, to note the profound changes in patterns of power and politics that the growing centrality of knowledge and its use are bringing about.

Many theorists of the knowledge society assume the ascendance of technocracy, that a "knowledge elite" of scientists, mathematicians, economists, engineers, and professionals of all sorts is progressively replacing traditional governing groups of managers, capitalists, and business executives. Even if they exaggerate this shift in power, their observations point to another key feature of the knowledge revolution as it has developed. Despite the democratic potential of knowledge, the explosion of knowledge and knowledge producing institutions has reinforced existing hierarchies and created new ones.

Technocracy's political qualities are hidden behind a stance of being "apolitical." Indeed, such concealment is sometimes promoted by champions of more engaged institutions. "Intellectual work that is driven by political forces is not intellectual at all," writes William Massy in *Honoring the Trust: Quality and Cost Containment in Higher Education*. Such politicized work, in his view, "seeks simply to win arguments and influence the distribution of power." He calls on the academy to rise above politics.

Values associated with this objective stance such as attention to method, respect for evidence, self-reflexivity, the need for diverse views, openness to feedback, and aspirations to excellence are important. Yet these are far better realized by conceiving of knowledge production as a relational public craft than by pretending detachment from politics or objectivity about the world. And of course, anyone who knows higher education knows how bizarre is the claim that it "rises above politics."

Massy's stance of apoliticality is the culmination of long-term trends that render technocracy at once invisible and omnipresent. These trends produced detachment as the characteristic stance in academia. They also are inextricably tied to the ways in which formal politics today functions as highly charged ideological warfare.

Technocratic patterns developed over many decades. "We all have to follow the lead of specialists," wrote Walter Lippmann at the end of World War I, who set much of the tone of intellectual life. He argued that a growing body of opinion "looks to the infusion of scientific method, the careful application of administrative technique." Science was the model for liberal thinking; technocrats the model actors. An editorial in *The New Republic* argued, "the business of politics has become too complex to be left to the pretentious misunderstandings of the benevolent amateur."

This pattern came to mean that academic knowledge produced by credentialed experts is what "counts," and the authority of those without formal credentials is systematically undermined. It detached professionals from the life of communities and eroded the civic cultures of organizations they direct. As citizens became clients and consumers, the process hollowed out the civic muscle of mediating institutions, from local unions to civically grounded schools, businesses, and voluntary associations. This dynamic has been a key reason for citizens' feelings of powerlessness.

In the early 1950s, Baker Brownell, a philosophy professor at Northwestern who had been involved in rural extension projects, described this pattern in a polemic against the academic world from which he came, decrying its role in spreading technocracy. "Truth is more than a report," he said. "It is an organization of values. Efficiency is more than a machine; it is a human consequence." Captivated by technique, procedure, method, and specialization, Brownell argued, the educated professional classes had lost sight of face-to-face relations. "It is the persistent assumption of those who are influential … that large-scale organization and contemporary urban culture can somehow provide suitable substitutes for the values of the human communities that they destroy," he declared.

> For want of a better word, I call these persons "the educated"—professionals, professors, businessmen, generals, scientists, bureaucrats, publicists, politicians, etc. They may be capitalist or they may be Communist in their affiliations, Christian or Jew, American, English, German, Russian or French. But below these relatively superficial variations among "the educated" there is a deeper affiliation. They are affiliated in the abstract, anonymous, vastly expensive culture of the modern city.

Brownell missed the multifold potential contributions of "the educated," when civically oriented and grounded, to a democratic society, but he had reason for targeting higher education as a cause of detachment and the erosion of communities. In *Academic Cultures in Transformation*, edited by Thomas Bender and Carl Schorske, leaders in four disciplines—economics, political science, philosophy, and English—document the growing detachment of academia from public life. Such detachment has shaped professional education, from business and engineering to ministry and teaching, resulting in the loss of interactive, horizontal ties to local civic life. As Bender put it in *Intellect and Public Life*, "In [the] largely successful quest for order, purity and authority, intellectuals severed intellectual life from place." A number of scholars and leaders in higher education have recently made similar points about the growing detachment of academic cultures over the last half-century.

When Edwin Fogelman and I interviewed senior faculty at the University of Minnesota in 1997 and 1998, we heard both about this detachment and its consequences. Leading faculty, from different disciplines, said that they consciously avoid mention of their public interests—what had led them into academia in the first place —for fear it might jeopardize their reputations for "rigorous scholarship." They feel increasingly cut off from local communities, or even their departmental communities, focused more on disciplinary or subdisciplinary reference groups. "I talk to 50 colleagues in my subfield by Internet far more than I talk to anyone on the hall," said one leading social scientist. Their discontents take shape in a silent politics whose authority comes from hiding interests and suppressing attachment to living communities.

In overt political terms, technocracy produces not only detached expertise but also a culture of critique and estrangement from middle-class Americans as the characteristic stance in higher education. The stance of critic, with its penchant for abstract and ideological categories, also has roots in the social movements of the later 1960s, with their sweeping posture of alienation from mainstream America, its symbols, stories, images, and traditions. Today, the stance of alienation is reflected in the labels that dominate on campuses —"corporations," "Christian fundamentalists," "Republicans," "whites," "males," and the like, on the side of oppressors, and categories like "oppressed minorities" and many others as innocent victims. More generally, the culture of critique generates a pervasively critical stance toward American society as a whole, with an implicit and almost entirely unreflected working assumption that "consciousness raising" about injustices and problems will somehow motivate young people to act constructively. When talking with students about what they have learned about broad American democratic traditions as sources of inspiration or what can be learned for constructive action from even failed efforts to address the failings of American society, we regularly hear enormous frustration about their lack of positive experiences. Many say they have rarely encountered positive views about American society from faculty members.

The politics of critique informs the work of leading definitions of "public scholarship" or "public intellectual" in higher education, as Scott Peters has shown. Moreover, as Dana Fisher demonstrates in *Activism, Inc.* a Manichean, "good-versus-evil" politics also structures the ways young people are introduced to political activism through techniques like the door-to-door canvass. In the door-to-door canvass, tens of thousands of young activists each year act out such politics in highly scripted ways. Canvassers are commanded like vast armies by groups like the Public Interest Research Foundation.

Daniel Patrick Moynihan once said, "The central conservative truth is that it is culture, not politics, that determines the success of a society," capturing how culture impacts politics. Moynihan also offered a redemptive alternative about politics' power. "The central liberal truth is that politics can change a culture and save it from itself." What does a culture-shaping politics look like? How can it be fostered?

The Politics of Public Work

Public work emphasizes what it is that citizens do, not only who citizens are, the *what* as well as the *who* of citizenship. It holds in tension the *is* and the *ought*; it brings together the human interests described by Jürgen Habermas—gritty, practical problem solving with communication and liberation. To effect such integration, the politics of public work poses three challenges to today's technocratic politics. First it explicitly counters expert takeover of politics and manipulations of mass sentiments by recovering citizen-centered politics attentive to the plurality and relationality of the human condition. Second, it challenges the distributive definition of politics by emphasizing the generative work of solving public problems and the catalytic role of professionals. Third, all this requires shifting the conceptual frame from the highly ideological politics of sweeping categories and Manichean sensibilities [1960s] to a strategic approach that excavates and builds on the democratic currents and values in communities and in the American society as a whole. The 1930s, especially the period of what was called the "Popular Front" to defend and deepen democracy against the dangers of fascism and cultural catastrophe, offers rich lessons for such a strategy.

In the first instance, the politics of public work builds on a tradition of theory and practice that has sought in recent decades to retrieve citizen-centered politics against the appropriation of politics by experts. Hannah Arendt pioneered in this retrieval. In *The Human Condition,* she describes public life as an environment of "innumerable perspectives and aspects in which the common world presents itself and for which no common measurement or denominator can ever be devised." It is a world of visibility and disclosure. "By their capacity for the immortal deed, by their ability to leave no perishable traces behind, men, their individual mortality notwithstanding, attain an immortality of their own and prove themselves to be of a 'divine' nature."

Today, intellectuals inside and outside the academy have begun to challenge technocracy with citizen-centered politics— Sheldon Wolin, David Mathews, Gerald Taylor, Mary Dietz, Rom Coles, Ernesto Cortes, and others. In citizen-centered terms, politics is primarily the free, horizontal interactions among equal citizens, and only secondarily their vertical relationships with politicians or the state. Citizen-centered politics disputes the expert takeover of political life. It differs from the manipulative mass politics of sweeping categories and clear-cut enemies that shape citizen activism, from Michael Moore movies or America Live radio to door-to-door canvassing and Internet mobilizations. Around the world, modern technologies of communications and mobilization whip up frenzied waves of activism, whether leftist protests against the World Bank, Arab protests against the pope, or right-wing protests against the removal of life support from Terri Shiavo. Public work politics is urgently needed to complicate every kind of abstract, categorical, idealized mode of thought. Such politics is rooted in the gritty soil of human plurality—the irreducibly particular stories, interests, and outlooks that each person brings to the public world.

Secondly, the politics of public work confounds the separation of work from political life and professions from civic culture. The stress on participation, central to activist or radical democratic theory, is an insufficient account of politics; participation can consign citizens to the role of consumers of government benefits, rather than emphasize their roles as producers of public goods and cocreators of civic life. Participation generally becomes channeled through participatory structures that do little to build living cultures. Public work highlights the productive, world-building aspects of politics, the need to solve public problems by bridging different interests and perspectives. It also suggests a generative understanding of power, not only power *over*, the dominant view, but power *to*, power that comes from creating public relationships, tapping new talent and imagination, and creating democratic cultures.

This brings into view a different concept of the role of professionals, shifting from a service-delivery model to catalytic and organizing roles. The tradition of democracy in the United States, understood as a way of life not simply formal institutions, has rich traditions in this vein. The distinctiveness of democracy in the United States, indeed, has been its tie to work. Democracy had resonance because citizens helped to make it, in its social, cultural, economic, as well as governmental, forms. In what David Mathews has called "the sweaty and muscular tradition of citizenship," citizens created civic communities full of public things, towns and town halls, schools and libraries, infrastructures, philanthropies, and cultural institutions. In the process they often gained an experience of equal citizenship.

> *"The emergence of a more robust concern with democracy recently reflects the effort to find a deeper rationale for institutions of higher education as actual places, living communities where people interact with each other in complex, multidimensional ways over time."*
>
> ("Public Work: An interview with Harry Boyte," *HEX*, 2000.)

These traditions became translated into the contemporary world in a myriad of ways. As the nation industrialized, civic populist intellectuals, such as Jane Addams, Liberty Hyde Bailey, James Weldon Johnson, Zora Neale Hurston, and others, played important roles in translating older ideas of productive labors to the new society by emphasizing the training of professionals for catalytic, energizing public work. Land-grant institutions made distinctive contributions to this process by explicit attention to the integration of practical with liberal education. Their robust sense of their civic role led to the designation of land-grants as "democracy's colleges."

Nick Bromell, professor of English at the University of Massachusetts in Amherst has well described the experience of positive freedom, equality, and abundance in public work. "It is through our work together that we most powerfully experience our equality with one another," Bromwell says.

Whether you are co-editing a volume of essays or organizing to keep a waste incinerator out of your neighborhood, cooperative labor means respectfully negotiating your differences and then collectively putting your shoulders to the wheel. It means listening and doing. It means allowing for the fullest possible play of individual ideas, methods, goals, and desires in order for the best of these to be selected without alienating your co-workers.

Creating relationships through real work of significance counters patterns of scarcity and isolation and credentialed expertise that dominate institutional life today.

Thirdly, a public work politics points toward a basic shift in the strategic framework of civic, social, and political alliances. Today's politics are set by the "left-versus-right" language and the sensibilities of the cultural and political wars of the 1960s and the subsequent ideological bent of disciplines structured around the intellectual roles of critic and outside expert. A more useful period to look at is the 1930s, for differences but also for lessons.

"No theory of the state is ever intelligible save in the context of its time," Harold Laski, the great theorist of the British Labor Party, began the fourth edition of *The Grammar of Politics*, in 1938. Laski and British Laborites shared the views of most American progressive intellectuals: democracy had external and internal enemies, alike. The rise of extremist forces in Europe and Japan threatened worldwide calamity. Internally, democracies faced economic crisis, the power of big business, and the loss of citizen confidence. All required unprecedented public

> *"I think the current emphasis of volunteerism 'dumbs down' citizenship by highlighting personal traits like caring and individual acts of kindness and eclipsing questions of power, collective action, the cultures and functioning of institutions, and larger systemic problems."*
>
> ("Public Work: An interview with Harry Boyte," *HEX*, 2000.)

action. In a striking example of this, the New Deal involved a renegotiation of the compact between citizens and government, in which "the American Way of Life" came to include many new social programs and governmental initiatives. Liberals in the United States as well as in Europe had enormous faith in government's capacities to advance social progress.

As in the 1930s, the nation today faces not only external threats like the growth of Islamic fundamentalism but also internal challenges. Real wages of nonsupervisory workers have stagnated for 30 years, while social benefits—most important, employer-based health insurance—have declined since 2000. We are surrounded by growing inequalities, huge technological transformations, fraying social ties, widespread feelings of powerlessness, and a materialistic, consumerist, hedonistic mass culture that celebrates dog-eat-dog competition.

Unlike the 1930s, intellectuals and the general public are far more skeptical about state action as the solution. Multiple studies, in the United States and around the world, have shown how expert-driven government action inattentive to local cultures can devastate communities. Republicans have had great success in charging, "I trust the people; my opponent trusts the government," as George W. Bush put it in 2000. It is unlikely that progressives in the 21st century will revive Laski's belief that government is "the keystone of the social arch." A more promising approach is a model of democratic governance in which the state is less a prime mover and more a catalyst for multiple social actors.

Here there are traditions of catalytic public action to draw on from the 1930s, parallel to the traditions of public professional work. Post offices, local schools, soil conservation districts, public work projects like the CCC and the WPA, and a host of other government bodies and initiatives played roles as civic catalysts and embedded civic centers of community life. As the research of civic scholars, such as Carmen Sirianni and Scott Peters, has demonstrated, these work-centered professional, land-grant, and governmental practices continue as vital subterranean traditions to recover and build upon in the making of a different paradigm of public action.

There are also important strategic lessons from the larger 1930s civic movement which we need to recall to counter the highly ideological patterns of today's politics. The New Deal electoral coalition played a role in meeting the nation's crisis, and government efforts were important, but the tone of the nation's collective response to the Great Depression was set by a larger movement, sometimes called the "Popular Front," against the dangers of fascism, that aimed at mobilizing civic energies across parties to meet the challenges. The Popular Front included a myriad of activities, from unionization of the auto industry and civil rights struggles to cultural work in film, theater, and journalism. It advanced democratic values like diversity, tolerance, equality, and the commonwealth, weaving "justice," the leitmotif of left-wing politics, into a broader repertoire of themes and practical projects. The "people," seen by intellectuals in the 1920s as the repository of crass materialism and parochialism, was rediscovered as the source of civic creativity. "The heart and soul of our country," said Franklin Roosevelt, "is the common man."

This 1930s civic renewal movement was infused with the spirit and practices of public work. And it depended on a shift in progressive thinking, which is parallel to the shift that needs to take place today on college campuses and in society. The unproductive "struggle for socialism" of the early 1930s had led to ferocious fights between radicals and moderates that bore resemblance to the divisions between leftists and centrists today. In the latter 1930s, the call for a Popular Front to *defend democracy* meant that broad alliances replaced demands to choose "which side are you on?" America's democratic heritage came to be understood as a treasure trove of cultural resources. Even the Communist Party claimed "Jefferson, Paine, Jackson, and Lincoln."

The Popular Front gave birth to a broad democratic aesthetic, illustrated by Martha Graham's 1938 dance masterpiece, *American Document*. It emphasized American folk traditions, multiethnic heritages, and ideals of the Declaration of Independence and the Gettysburg Address. "What is an American?" she asked. She answered, not only Anglo-Saxons but also blacks, immigrants, and

workers. All were needed for democracy. The appeal of Earl Robin-
son's great song on the same theme and with the same message,
"Ballad for Americans," showed the reach of this democratic aesthetic. Made famous by Paul Robeson, in 1940 it was sung at the
conventions of both the Republican and the Communist parties.

We need a similar reconfiguring of cultural and political energies and strategic thinking if we are to advance the civic mission
of higher education and locate that effort in the larger movement
for democratic revitalization. There are fledgling signs of such a
movement, described in a new Case Foundation study, *Citizens at
the Center*, by Cindy Gibson, charting promising trends that regen-
erate a civic ethos or culture of citizenship. *Citizens at the Center* does
not explicitly address the role of higher education in this movement.
But it is possible to do so from a public work perspective.

Public Work in Higher Education

> The world is deluged with panaceas, formulas, pro-
> posed laws, machineries, ways out, and myriads of
> solutions. It is significant and tragic that almost every
> one of these proposed plans and alleged solutions
> deals with the structure of society, but none concerns
> the substance—the people. This, despite the eternal
> truth of the democratic faith that the solution always
> lies with the people.
>
> *Saul Alinsky,* Reveille for Radicals, *1946*

Alinsky here gave a vivid description of the way technocratic
politics replaces "the democratic faith" with "myriads of solutions."
His alternative was drawn from the experiences of Popular Front
organizing. Indeed, his first book, *Reveille for Radicals*, can be seen
as a powerful statement of such organizing. For example, in his
chapter on community traditions, Alinsky argues that the task of
the organizer in any community is not to "convert" or divide along
ideological lines. Rather, the organizer must engage in a deep
process of listening to community values, traditions, mores, and
habits. Organizing is about bringing forth the democratic potentials
that exist in any community. I experienced this democratic politics
rooted in the Popular Front directly as a young man, working as a

field secretary for the Southern Christian Leadership Conference. SCLC's strategic frame was set especially by Ella Baker and Bayard Rustin, with roots in the 1930s. Its politics—full of alliance building and efforts to mine the symbols, images, and cultures of diverse democratic and religious traditions—was sharply different than the politics of caution typified by the NAACP, or the politics of alienation in the left wing of the movement.

The challenge today is to revive the organizing skills, the professional sensibilities, and the larger strategic framework of the 1930s and their continuing legacy in SCLC and broad-based community organizing. We also need to adapt these for a radically different age. There is no quick fix but there are many things to build on in higher education.

For instance, service learning over the last two decades has spread across the landscape of higher education because it creates democratic practices and more engagement—relational cultures, pedagogies, and approaches to knowledge; alternatives to academic norms; and practices of detachment. Many faculty whom I have interviewed describe service learning as a life-changing source of rejuvenation of public purpose. Because it focuses on integrating disciplinary knowledge with real-life experiences far beyond faculty control, service learning creates alternatives to detached one-way pedagogies. Service learning is tied to new views of public scholarship such as community-based or participatory action research in which community knowledge is understood to be valuable and students are coproducers of knowledge. Imagining America, the consortium of schools dedicated to promoting the public work of faculty in humanities, arts, and design fields, explicitly is taking up the theme of organizing for culture change in higher education and beyond.

Other trends also suggest the signs of what might be called a paradigm shift. In social theory, the concept of "social capital," with its relational, communal associations has replaced an individualist and economic emphasis on "human capital." In experimental psychology, new research emphasizes humans as unique agents of their own development. Thus, for instance, the late child-development

scientist Esther Thelen pioneered in developing a "grand unify-
ing theory" of the field. Her approach was based on a relational,
interactive, emergent understanding of complex systems and
how to theorize them. In her view the scientist herself is part of
the equation. Theory grows not only from use of the scientific
method but also from a rich and interactive set of plural relationships, with "amateurs" as well as other scientists. Thelen's
theory has challenged views of infants as passing through predetermined "stages" of development to understanding infants to
be experimental and self-realizing agents, profoundly relational
and interactive with their context. In development work, new
theory challenges technocratic, one-size-fits-all interventions.
Thus, the recent volume edited by Vijayendra Rao and Michael
Walton, *Culture and Public Action*, drawn from UN and World Bank
experiences around the world, is a case in point. Through case
studies and cultural theory, contributors develop an overwhelming critique of technocratic and ideological approaches that have
dominated. They call for work that is respectful of, knowledgeable
about, and skilled in negotiating with local cultures in development literature and practice.

This shift is from "structural thinking" to "citizen thinking,"
and from ideological politics to broad alliance building politics.
Structures and institutions are neither the solution to complex
public problems nor our enemies, but rather our tools. Citizens
need to be at the center. And today's categories like "conservative,"
"liberal," or "left" are far less useful than a detailed mapping, as
Alinsky once put it, of what makes for "constructive democratic
action" and what impedes or opposes such action.

Building on positive developments, here are three ingredients
for transforming the technocratic and ideological politics that stifles
democratic energies in higher education and the larger society:
we need political education that challenges abstractions and
teaches work attentive to context and particularities of interests
and backgrounds. We need organizing for cultural change in our
professions and institutions to reground them in living contexts.
And we need a broader political and strategic framework that

shifts scholarly attention from what is wrong to the primary question, what solves problems in ways that build democratic society?

Unfreezing politics. The first shift needed is from politics as highly professionalized, ideological warfare to an understanding of politics as the interplay and negotiation of diverse interests to create a common civic life and to advance democratic values and tendencies. Developments in higher education suggest possibilities for bringing such citizen-centered politics into our institutions. These draw on what is called "broad-based citizen organizing," in large citizen networks like the Industrial Areas Foundation, the Gamaliel Foundation, and PICO.

Building substantial power for ordinary people—the core mission of these organizations—involves a molecular organizing process of empowerment that requires people learning how to form public relationships with others who are profoundly different. This means creating cultures of a different kind of politics.

For 18 years, the Hubert H. Humphrey Institute of Public Affairs' Center for Democracy and Citizenship and its collaborators have developed initiatives that show the possibilities for spreading democratic populist politics in varied settings, especially in schools and higher education itself. In Public Achievement, a youth civic engagement pedagogy developed by the Center for Democracy and Citizenship, teams of young people, ranging from elementary to high school students, work over months on a public issue they choose. They are coached by adults, who help them develop achievable goals and learn political skills and political concepts. Teams address a large range of issues, including teen pregnancy, racism, violence, and school curriculum. A variety of studies show often-remarkable accomplishments. In 2004 to 2005 about 3000 young people were involved in Public Achievement in more than 80 sites in a number of American communities. It has also spread to a dozen other countries, including Turkey, Scotland, Palestine, and Poland.

The pedagogies of Public Achievement have also been translated into other settings with students and professionals. The leadership minor at the University of Minnesota and James Farr's political science course, organized around Public Achievement, has spawned a student initiative, the Student Committee on Public Engagement, SCOPE, dedicated to culture change at the university, "producing citizens not partisans," as one student put it, developing far deeper emphasis on public engagement, community, and public work. We are now seeing considerable interest among these students in the earlier, buried history and strategic lessons of the 1930s, as an alternative to the Red-Blue warfare that dominates on campuses today.

Public work politics has also proven valuable in professional practice. Indeed, complex problems are rarely discrete phenomena around which generic professional interventions can be mounted successfully if one is attentive to overall community well-being. With a focus on organizing for culture change, "problems" come to be understood as interconnected—lead poison in housing may be tied to the jobs that require people to live in certain areas, for instance. They are also woven into the life of civic communities. Thus they are different in every community, requiring distinctive approaches that take account of local cultures, with their unique histories, networks, capacities, and identities.

In Tomah, Wisconsin, in a collaborative project called Communities Mobilized for Change on Alcohol with the University of Minnesota's department of epidemiology on teenage alcohol use, we found that a focus on public work transformed public health practices while developing new approaches to collaboration and public leadership development. The customary approach of public health, in which "evidence-based interventions" focus on policy change to deal with a particular health problem, shifted to strategies based on changing the civic culture.

To accomplish this shift, Jeanne Carls, the organizer in Tomah, created a strategy team with diverse groups and interests who had never worked together and did not agree on the definition of "the problem." Yet all agreed that something was wrong, after several teenage deaths in alcohol-related incidents. Police, bar owners, merchants, church leaders, teenagers, parents, and public-health professionals became involved. "You tell people that there are going to be many different people coming together who you may have thought would never be at the same table, but can see the need to work on the same issue," Carls recounted. "It was like bringing lions to the table. People would sit across the table and never talk to each other directly, but they all had an interest in youth, and in Tomah." Health-care workers, city officials, and lay citizens worked to define what the problem entailed. What emerged was a view of teenage alcohol use as inextricably tied to the civic culture of Tomah as a whole community. They realized that the annual festival, in which beer drinking was the central ritual for people of all ages, was both a symbol and wellspring of the town's drinking culture. All were responsible for the problem, understood in this fashion. And many different groups would be required to change it. Such a change also entailed a shift in professional practices from one-way policy interventions to collaborative public work. "I bring some specific skills and knowledge, like how things are decided in city politics," said Dave Berner, the city manager. "But many others make contributions as well." Work on teen alcohol abuse resulted in Berner's rethinking his job in far more civic ways.

Organizing for citizen professionalism. An organizing approach in higher education is different than approaches to change based on dissemination of information, service delivery, or moralized protest. It engages people through their diverse interests, builds alliances that take account of power relationships and institutional cultures, and has a strong, relational approach. Maria Avila, a former Mexican American organizer with the Industrial Areas Foundation who directs the Center for Community Based Learning at Occidental College, describes elements of an organizing approach in higher education. "The medicine for our predicament requires efforts to restructure the way we think, act, behave toward each other, and the way we act as a collective to restructure power and resources." Avila argues that organizing focuses on culture change. "Culture changes [come] first, leading to structural changes later."

We have seen the potential of using such an organizing approach and also the conception of "citizen professional" reintegrated into living civic cultures in a number of settings. In the early 1990s, for instance, Project Public Life (the CDC's precursor at the Humphrey Institute) undertook a Citizen Politics initiative in Minnesota with Minnesota Extension that helped to unearth older traditions of public work and everyday politics in the cooperative extension system in the state and across the nation, creating the background for the pioneering historical scholarship of Scott Peters. The effort also showed that substantial civic renewal initiatives with statewide associations require an organizing approach, not informational or programmatic approaches. Organizing with Minnesota Extension Services meant seeking to build sustained capacities for collective citizen action in and around extension. The effort depended on creating a statewide leadership team led by MES director Pat Borich, a populist who had come up through the extension ranks, as well as local leadership teams. It involved cultivating new capacities for deliberation and public work. It aimed at changing the culture of the bureaucracy so it would be more responsive to local communities, more aware of citizen capacities, and more flexible in giving local extension agents room for innovation.

Other developments in the University of Minnesota also explicitly seek to effect culture changes that counter the detached technocratic biases of service delivery. For instance, the Academic Health Center (AHC) at the UMN has established a new Citizen Health Care Program, building on the work of William Doherty and his colleagues. This is framed by the public work approach, explicitly challenging the technocratic "service delivery" model of health care, aimed at teaching professionals across the country a new model of collaborative work. This means reconceptualizing themselves as citizens working with other citizens. As its founding statement puts it, Citizen Health Care is:

> based on the belief that the greatest untapped resource for improving health care is the knowledge, wisdom, and energy of individuals, families, and communities who live with challenging health issues in their everyday lives. In this approach, health care professionals learn public skills for working with patients who are citizens of health care, builders of health in clinic and community, rather than consumers of medical services.

At the AHC, cultural change is also sometimes prompted by initiatives from outside. Thus, the Academic Health Center also has a partnership with the Powderhorn Wellness Center initiated by community leader Atum Azzahir. This partnership immerses residents in the cultures and traditional healing practices of a low-income community, as a part of their education. Azzahir describes her own shift more than a decade ago from what she calls the "oppression framework" focused on attacking white racism, to the "cultural reconstruction" approach, based on deep exploration, retrieval, and affirmation of relational and soulful elements in the cultures of people of African descent. Her approach combines a deep grounding in the civic life of communities with an affirmation of the vital role that culture identity plays as a source of strength and healing.

Finally, we have developed organizing efforts at culture change in geographic areas. Thus, the Jane Addams School for Democracy, a learning and public work partnership in the West Side neighborhood of St. Paul with new immigrant communities from Asia, Africa, and Latin America, which has involved more than 1000 students from the University of Minnesota since 1997, has a focus on creating a democratic, relational culture across the neighborhood. Students learn to think of themselves as "members" of the Jane Addams School, not as students doing "service projects." The theme is that "everyone is a learner and everyone is a teacher." This creates an experience of colearning, cocreation, and grassroots public leadership development. It also has renewed the idea of education tied to the civic life of places. Jane Addams School has helped to spawn a neighborhood-wide initiative, the Neighborhood Learning Community, in which the whole community and its institutions—from parents to congregations, libraries, businesses, and community organizations—have claimed authority for the education of children. Its mission is to create a neighborhoodwide learning culture. Many new forms of collaboration have emerged. For instance, an apprenticeship program connects teenagers with local employers, with a strong reflective component. All Around the Neighborhood has produced a collaboration of diverse groups to educate children in different topics, from science to neighborhood history.

The Neighborhood Learning Community points toward a sharply different policy approach based on abundance, or the vast untapped energies now frozen by technocratic politics. In Minnesota today, as elsewhere in the United States, progressive reformers in politics, business, higher education, and education use a scarcity frame, defining the problem as growing disparities along lines of income, education, housing, and other public goods.

In fact, the traditional strength of Minnesotan education was the way in which schools were connected to civic life. This tie was in fact enshrined in the state's distinctive policy innovations, such as community education and early childhood family education, run through community boards. The erosion of this connection, with a resulting view of education based on scarcity, dramatizes the need for alternatives.

Advancing democratic society. Technocracy, the expert stance outside a common life, seeking to manipulate the world, sustains academic practices as well as professions as self-referential, abstract, and full of techniques, devoid of public life. Schools, social service agencies, and other civic institutions, whether in Buenos Aires or Minneapolis, are often as detached from local cultures as are fast-food businesses and Wal-Marts. Yet many trends in higher education and other settings challenge the privatizing and scarcity-based dynamics of technocracy. Democratic society, rather than democratic state, entails a fundamentally different conception of the academic and intellectual's role, a shift from critic and outsider to engaged intellectual who helps generate constructive action. See the following chart on the contrast, developed by Marie Ström of the Institute for Democracy in South Africa, who has translated public work concepts into the South African context.

To renew democracy in these terms entails creating an alternative politics based on abundance, not scarcity. It means seeing ourselves as intellectuals as part of the world, not detached from it. It involves teaching the habits and skills of democratic citizenship, as well as the skills of organizing for social change. And it requires understanding our institutions not as ivory towers but as engaged in changing the world as well. Our fate is bound up with that of everyone else.

Identity	Moving from "Democratic State" to "Democratic Society": Our Work as Intellectuals	
	Expert/critic/ commentator	Intellectual leader/catalyst
Definition of democracy	Democratic state	Democratic society
Definition of citizen	Consumer, client, voter, individual with rights; spectator of politics	Cocreator, problem solver
Purpose of work as intellectuals	Analyze policy; express opinion; critique existing society	Stimulate a conversation; challenge "the world as it is" in order to help create a new sense of possibility beyond the given
Stance	Detached, objective	Engaged; "part of the mix"
Core work	Gather, analyze, and disseminate information	Build relationships; stimulate public discussion; activate and energize
Responsibility	Highlight injustice and inequality; speak on behalf of the voiceless; promote "fix it" policies	Expand public space; advocate for policies that empower the people and build civic energy
Relationships and sphere of work	Sectoral/disciplinary/ "in-group," self-referential/ "enclosed space"	Strategic partnerships to stimulate and expand discussion; "public space"
Content and outcomes	Activities (statements, interviews, articles, submissions, events, and so on)	Action (strategic interventions in alliance with others to promote system change)
Methods	Reports, studies, Power Point presentations, Web sites, databases	Building relationships, tapping diverse interests, creating alliances
Evaluation	Numbers (events, beneficiaries, and so on)	Impact (shift in discourse; change in attitudes, people, or capacity)

Our broadest challenge of higher education is to advance democratic values and to join in movements to build citizen-centered democratic societies. This is the only real way to bring professionals, who see themselves often as outsiders, back into a common civic life. It is also how, together, we will develop the civic power to guide a world spinning out of control.

Public Work at Colgate: An Interview with Adam Weinberg

David Brown, coeditor of the Higher Education Exchange, *spoke with Adam Weinberg, Dean of the College at Colgate University and a professor of sociology, to learn more about the ongoing story of "public work" as it has emerged at Colgate.*

Brown: To start off, Adam, can you describe the work that you have been doing at Colgate?

Weinberg: It has been a seven-year process to rebuild campus life at Colgate around principles of civic learning. We started by getting about 400 students involved in a partnership with the local community around economic development. We did everything from work on a microenterprise program to help develop a "buy local" campaign. That work led to about $15 million of investment in the local community. We then launched an innovative community center to move students from thin forms of service to deeper forms of team-based community work.

Based on lessons learned from the community work, we launched our residential education program, which has gotten a lot of national attention. The basic idea was to "capture all the educational moments" that take place as students' time on campus. We have focused on capturing the civic potential in residential halls, student organizations, and other forms of everyday life.

It is really a very simple concept. Rather than getting students to go through a one-size-fits-all program, we asked ourselves: What are students doing outside the classroom? What do students want to do? Can we tweak those things just a little to give them some educational value? To get to this place, we have focused on getting students to do what Harry Boyte and others call "public work." Harry has a great quote in his last book where he calls for educational institutions to develop with young people the capacities and interest to work with others to "negotiate diverse interests for the sake of creating things with broad public benefit." This requires creating a more entrepreneurial campus culture where students would think of themselves as innovators, creators, and problem solvers. It required us to change our approach to campus life trying to find civic learning in every corner of students' daily lives.

Brown: You mentioned getting national attention. What is the significance of the work you describe?

Weinberg: We started from the observation that students lead busy lives outside the classroom, but we do not do a good job of capturing the educational value in those activities. Partially, this comes about because colleges and universities use professionalized models, where people solve problems for students. For example: residential halls are filled with layers of professional staff who spend their time solving problems by enforcing an endless stream of rules. If a student has a roommate conflict he calls the Office of Residential Life and a professional staff will find the proper rule or procedure to solve the problem. This is a horrible way to organize an educational environment. We rob students of opportunities to learn through problem solving. We reinforce notions of entitlements as students come to see college staff as service providers and themselves as customers or guests.

At Colgate, we have moved away from a professional service model by infusing campus with the spirit of public work. We want students to think of themselves as members of a community who have a responsibility to work with others to create a healthy living environment. We are then working with them to make sure that they have the organizing skills to act on their public values.

In my view, there are a few important shifts embedded in this view: first, we are arguing that we need to give students a more robust definition of democracy that moves beyond democracy as voting and community service to democracy as a way of life. To get to this place, we need to capture all the educational moments. Civic education takes place in campus controversies, residential halls, student organizations, campus planning, and a range of other places. Finally, we are challenging people to move beyond values. We need to make sure that our students have the skills and habits to act on their values.

Brown: Where has the most exciting or surprising work taken place at Colgate?

Weinberg: Definitely residential halls. I came up through the service-learning moment. I was fixated on getting students out of the residential halls and into the community. It never occurred to me that residential halls were equally good settings to teach the arts of democracy.

Take the typical residential hall—we pack a diversity of students into small spaces. Ninety per cent of these students have never shared a room with another person. Likewise, the diversity in each hall grows as students become more diverse by race, ethnicity, sexual orientation, AOD (alcohol and other drug) issues, and a range of other categories. As this occurs, the halls become filled with disagreement and conflict. Too often we approach these conflicts as if we were running hotels or resorts. We see problems as things to be avoided or solved.

Instead, we have learned to use conflicts as opportunities to help students learn to do public work. We have redefined the role of our residential advisors, or RAs, (student staff who live on each hall). Rather than being police officers who enforce rules or professionalized staff who solve problems, we want them to think of themselves as coaches and mentors who organize teams of students to tackle problems and/or take advantage of opportunities. We have also created community councils in each residential unit where students learn how to organize others, how to identify problems and opportunities, and how to brainstorm solutions through social action.

One of my favorite stories occurred in a freestanding college house where students were organizing a co-op dining plan. Conflict broke out because everybody left their dirty dishes in a sink. In the old student services model, an RA would have developed and imposed a set of rules on the house. It would not have worked. The RA would have been demoralized and the community would have fallen apart. In the new model, we replaced the RA with a community coordinator (a student) who is basically a community organizer. The community coordinator brought everybody together and led a group brainstorming session that resulted in a creative solution. The group went to the local hardware store, bought a piece of Styrofoam and placed it in half of the sink, which left no place for students to dump the dirty dishes. The students did public work. They worked across difference to solve a problem that had lasting social value. They also learned that community starts in the small democratic actions that people take in the everyday.

Brown: And student organizations, what about them?

Weinberg: Our campus is filled with 130+ student organizations that produced thousands of potential educational moments for students to learn important civic skills like mobilizing peers, facilitating a meeting, creating an action plan, working in teams, and resolving conflicts. We were capturing virtually none of those moments. If you walked around campus at night, you would see people involved in student organizations that did not work. Meetings were poorly planned. Organizations lacked mission statements, much less action plans for the semester. Minor conflicts led to splintering of groups. Not surprisingly most groups were fixated on developing programs that were ill conceived. Tactics never matched goals, and resources were usually poorly aligned with actions. This also had negative macrocampus effects, as student organizations divided students into tiny identity groups. Whereas we wanted student organizations to become places for students to "walk across difference" (meet different kinds of people), student organizations became mechanisms for creating comfort zones.

We created a Center for Leadership and Student Involvement and hired great mentors who could work with students to transform campus organizations into civic educational experiences. We started by changing how students think about student organizations. Rather than thinking in terms of activities, we have gotten students to think about themselves as community organizations that drive campus life. We started focusing heavily on training and skills development. We run an organizing summit before classes start. We help student organizations to work as a team to produce action plans for events, which include goals, strategies, and tactics. We use alumni, parents, and local community members to teach students to plan meetings, facilitate conversations, and to work through conflict.

We also created new funding mechanisms to encourage students to organize, plan, and work across difference. For example: we started a program called Breaking Bread through which students can access a pool of money to fund a wide variety of events. There is only one caveat: students have to plan the event with a group of students with whom they normally do not interact. They plan the event over dinner. The groups work together to create the menu, shop, cook, set up, and clean up. The outcome of the dinner is a series of objectives that the groups want to work together to accomplish together. In other words, they "break bread" together and plan events that will make the campus more vibrant and robust with regards to race and ethnic issues. They do public work by learning to walk across difference to be cocreators of public goods. For example: Sisters of the Round Table (women of color) and Rainbow Alliance (Lesbian, Gay, Bisexual, Transgender, Queer or Questioning) did some great work together. So did the College Republicans and the Muslim Student Association.

Brown: Going back in time for a moment, who specifically formulated the strategic objectives ("residential education for democracy")? How long did it take?

Weinberg: It was a community-based process. We spent a year talking about civic learning. At first, the conversations were formal planning/visioning conversations, but the circles were wide and the conversations were open-ended. People had space to talk across the community in ways that typically had not happened before. Our psychologists, administrative deans, campus safety officers, career service staff, and others spent hours sharing ideas about concepts and theories of democracy and civic education. We then organized another set of conversations to bring student affairs staff together with faculty and students. For example: a group of students, faculty, and administrators met weekly to talk about building civic life as a way to deal with alcohol issues.

All of this started to generate excitement and optimism that new things were possible. The circle widened beyond the formal conversations. A series of informal conversations emerged. These conversations were organic, but connected to the formal conversations in overt and subtle ways. New participants, including more students and faculty, were invited to join. These conversations became places to test ideas, refine concepts, and find new participants. The end product was an on-campus community of students, faculty, and administrators thinking about, defining, and developing new ways to deepen civic learning.

Brown: Was there anything about Colgate's culture that made it resistant?

Weinberg: Absolutely. Most of the resistance was generational. This generation of students and parents see entitlements, not responsibilities. They think about college as purchasing a set of services for my child to make them happy and professionally successful. Of course, we are moving in a different direction.

As I said earlier, this generation has great values, but they lack the skills to act on those values. Who would be surprised given the ways families and communities organize childhood? Everything has become structured and professionalized—which is the surest way to kill creativity and innovation and teamwork —which are the hallmarks of public work. We have a generation that doesn't like confrontation or conflict. They either avoid conflict or hold firm to polarized views, much like we see on talk radio. They also have a hard time holding each other accountable. They work better when other people organize them and set expectations. This generation has too many umbrella parents who are extending adolescence far into adulthood while also narrowing how young people come to define the purpose of education and the value of civic life.

Brown: Given their professional aspirations (and their parents for them) and the high cost of a private university, why would students be interested in developing habits of citizenship in their residence halls and other venues?

Weinberg: In the abstract, it is easy. People are wiser and care much more than we give them credit for. There is a great cynicism about Americans that I don't understand. People care about democracy. They understand that places like Colgate have a civic mission and that colleges and universities need to produce citizens.

People push back when we tell them that we are not going to solve a problem, but want their son/daughter to learn to problem solve with others. I would argue that 70 percent of our parents love it and deeply understand why we do it. Thirty percent would rather we not, but they understand the rationale. Eighty percent still push when it is about their child, but we have gotten very good at explaining the philosophy.

For example: a parent will call us because their son/daughter is being kept up by a roommate. We explain that this is a great opportunity for their son/daughter to learn how to get along with people and to negotiate space—a fundamental skill of democracy. A parent will respond by saying that they don't care about civic skills, they sent their child to college to get good grades so they can get a good job. We spend lots of time trying to help parents reexamine why we provide young people with an education— especially a liberal arts education.

Of course, there is an irony. Civic skills are also great life skills. While we are focused on students learning to run a meeting, work with others, negotiate conflicts, do planning, parents also understand these to be skills that will make them professionally successful.

I think we grossly underestimate how much Americans want educational institutions to be relevant politically and civically. We tend to sell ourselves for the economic impact—we produce good workers and students who can fill jobs. Politically, higher education would garner more national attention if we resold ourselves as institutions that will produce citizens who can lead communities.

Brown: Changing any organization's culture is difficult and time consuming. Does the four-year window you have for most students make that even harder?

Weinberg: Four years is fine. It would be better if students came to college a bit later and/or came with a richer set of life experiences, walking across difference and taking responsibility for themselves and others. I would advocate for a year, or two, of national service for every student in either the military or AmeriCorps. I would love to see colleges like Colgate give admissions points to students who take a year off and do something independent.

It would also help if students came to college with a set of life experiences dealing with diversity. Too many students are growing up in very homogeneous environments. Students are growing up in very diverse metropolitan regions with remarkably homogeneous sets of life experiences. They live in neighborhoods, attend schools, and do structured activities with kids like themselves. To compound the problem, they tend to be in smaller families where everybody has their own room and "stuff." Finally, given the way we structure childhood, adults make sure that the kids who do not get along are on different teams, in a different classroom. All of this means that really wonderful young people come to college lacking the experiences it takes to live democratically (working with others, negotiating conflict, walking across difference).

Brown: Was it particularly hard for students already there compared to entering students?

Weinberg: Yes. Change is hard. This generation does not like change. They are working hard to create small friendship networks as a way to re-create the "safe communities" that their parents created for them growing up. This generation is part of a rapidly changing world and they will need the skills to negotiate that world.

Brown: You have moved students from individual service opportunities to group problem solving. Have there been "unintended consequences" in such a shift, either on campus or with local communities?

Weinberg: Sure. Students wind up mobilizing against the local power structure—which is me! Students also solve problems in ways that have unintended consequences for others. The campus becomes filled with conflict, controversy. It just all becomes messy. You have to learn to embrace and love it.

Brown: Given what you and others have done at Colgate, has it had any measurable effect on the recruitment and retention of students? Of faculty? Of staff?

Weinberg: Residential education allowed us to think anew about old problems. It also sent a message that we were going to take ourselves more seriously, wade into the middle of national conversations, be relevant and a bit edgy, and try to lead the country. This had a huge impact across the university. Admissions applications were up 20 percent last year. This is a huge leap and more than peer schools. We yielded really well the last two years. We suspect that we are becoming a hot school within important pipelines for us.

We have also had two great fundraising years. Fundraising is changing. Younger alumni are more investment oriented. They want to make sure that their dollars have an impact. We are finding that our alumni increasingly care about civic learning. They are worried about the lack of civil discourse in America and the global challenges and opportunities for democracy. They are excited about residential education. We are getting great applications for student affairs jobs. Most student affairs people know the professionalized service model does not work. They are excited to come to a place that is building campus life around principles of civic learning.

Brown: Getting back to your observation that most students come to Colgate having never shared a room with anyone, having led very structured lives organized by their parents and other adults, and having grown up in homogeneous neighborhoods. If these are obstacles for what you and others are trying to change at Colgate, does this mean that the mix of those recruited and admitted will undergo change too?

Weinberg: I hope not. I don't want Colgate to become a success through skimming. Or put more crassly, I don't want to put the hoop over the dog (as opposed to teaching the dog to jump through the hoop.) Colgate attracts great students, many of whom will go on to make a difference in the world. The problem is not the students. The challenge is to take students who have grown up in noncivic communities, and to equip them with the capacity and skills to be citizens, community organizers, and democratic leaders.

Brown: When you speak of administrators, staff, and residential advisors getting out of the way and letting students take responsibility for the problems that arise among them, do they and the students really accept and live with whatever outcomes emerge?

Weinberg: It is a dance. Like democracy, it is messy and a negotiated process that never ends. We are living with things that we don't like but we also place boundaries. For example: we have a row of freestanding houses. It is our old fraternity row. Some of the houses are fraternities, others are theme houses, sororities, or new entrepreneurial houses. Last year, we encouraged the students to create a Broad Street Community Council to self-govern the program. We focused them around notions of public work and created a venture social fund they could use to encourage innovation and creativity. In some ways, the BSCC is working on issues in ways that I wouldn't choose—some of the solutions are just too formalized. But, we continue to be supportive and to let them organize in ways that they deem valuable. We keep telling them "here are nine different ways to do something." You can pick one of the 9, or invent a 10th. We are clear that they need a way, but we will support their choice. But we will only do it within boundaries. We are working hard to get students to see democracy as governance, not government. We don't want students on Broad Street to reduce self-governance to electing a council that does things for them. We want every student on Broad Street to see democracy as a way of life, and the council as a resource for groups of students who want to come together to do public work.

Brown: Faculty involvement seems to have been an important part of all that you and others have done. Given the habits and priorities of faculty, have there been significant changes in the degree of their participation?

Weinberg: Yes. More faculty are aware of what we are doing and helpful in articulating the message and support with students. And more faculty are involved in programs and (more important) in planning. We created two teams of faculty, student-affairs staff, and coaches. One is focused on the first-year experience and one is focused on the sophomore-year experience. They are trying to ensure that we are thinking broadly across the totality of what we are doing. We also have faculty heavily involved in other programs. A few have even offered to live in our residential halls!

Perhaps the most important involvement has been the very informal ways faculty mentor students. As one would expect, our faculty spend lots of time with students in their offices talking about all sorts of things. As part of this, faculty have been really important in helping change the culture. One of the hardest parts of the shift is getting students to understand a changed set of expectations for college life. Faculty are involved in helping explain the message.

It is also interesting, however, that faculty have not driven this process. There is a division of labor that works for us. There is a lot of "chatter" in the higher education community about getting faculty reengaged in the "out of the classroom" experience. I am not sure that this needs to be a priority for doing civic education. I don't think that we need to return to a mythic version of 1950. A lot of this is driven by changes that are good. Faculty have working spouses. Faculty are engaged in research that really matters to moving society forward. I would argue that we need faculty to worry about how to do civic education through the classroom with more engaged pedagogies (e.g. problem-based learning, service learning, community-based research). We need student affairs folks to worry about doing this through things like residential programs and student organizations. And we need student affairs and academic affairs leaders (e.g. administrators and faculty idea entrepreneurs) to be talking/coordinating with each other.

Brown: Are you saying, that with more nonacademic professionals available, that they are better at "doing civic education" than faculty members?

Weinberg: No. Nothing works better than service learning. The data collected by Campus Compact, the National Survey on Student Engagement, and others is very clear on this point. I would argue that faculty should be doing it in the classroom. And student-affairs folks should be doing it through campus life. It should be coordinated, but a division of labor is okay. We should be comfortable with it. It is Community Organizing 101—everybody has a role and those roles should be coordinated.

Brown: Assuming that Colgate, like most other institutions of higher education, operates in a "conflicted state of educational values and priorities," how have such conflicts affected the work that you have undertaken there with others?

Weinberg: There are all sorts of tensions. Faculty want to do service learning, but they also have time constraints. It is also true with parents and their visions for what we should be doing. We get some interesting push back from alumni who view our programs as social engineering when, in reality, we are giving students more control than they had under the old models. And there are always battles over allocation of resources.

Brown: When we spoke earlier you said that it is easy to justify civic education within the context of the liberal arts. If so, why then has the classroom been a problem?

Weinberg: Part of it is real. Faculty have multiple demands on their time. They have lots of competing needs for the classroom. Part of it is new. We are just starting to understand the power of engaged pedagogies. That requires constructing structures with incentives to help faculty stay on the cutting-edge of teaching.

But part of it is also less real, or self-imposed in destructive ways. Too many faculty have professionalized themselves. They see themselves as a narrow type of scientist. My father was a scientist. I often find it odd that many faculty in the social sciences are trying to be a sort of scientist that most scientists would not want to be. Great civic education comes from faculty who think about themselves, their work, and their teaching in much more craftlike ways. My discipline (sociology) may be the worst. As we become more professionalized we have less to offer students and more irrelevant to larger public conversations. Given the history of sociology, we should see lots of sociologists interested in civic education and/or service learning. Instead, sociologists are scared that it will make them seem "weak" or "not a real scientist."

Brown: Is there feedback from faculty members that what the university is encouraging students to do outside the classroom is affecting what's going on inside their classrooms?

Weinberg: Sure.… There are two sorts of murmurs in the system: (1) it detracts from academic work, and (2) some students are not joiners. But, this is really a small group. Most faculty are concerned that campus culture not be anti-intellectual. A focus on civic learning reignites an intellectual feel, a robustness and vibrancy that is essential for a learning environment. Also, civic learning is consistent with the liberal arts. It is all about innovation, creativity, and problem solving.

Brown: Why was the campus culture "anti-intellectual"?

Weinberg: Largely it is a national problem. Too many students come to college either fixated on careers (and thus they are purely consumers who want to know the facts they need to memorize in order to get a good grade) or looking for a four-year vacation filled with parties (see Tom Wolfe's most recent book). We are not serious enough about education. We don't ask enough of our students. And our students don't ask enough of themselves. Ironically, some of the most serious campuses that I have been on are community colleges and/or tier-three public institutions, where students are coming desperate for an education. We have worked hard to make Colgate a more serious place and it is working. Our civic education work was a key component of that strategy.

Brown: Obviously in any initiative, such as the one we are discussing, the self-interest of the institution is heavily engaged. Has that self-interest been adequately served by what has happened in the local communities and on campus? For example, have such initiatives affected the "status" concerns of alumni, which you note in your "The University: An Agent of Social Change" piece?

Weinberg: In huge ways. The transformation of the Village has been so positive for Colgate. More alumni come back to campus for weekends. They are proud of Colgate and Hamilton. We used to hear prospective students complain about the Village, now they talk about it as a draw.

Brown: Are there dissenting opinions, and, if so, what are their concerns?

Weinberg: Yes. People will argue that there is too much emphasis on student affairs, cynicism about students (can this really work). But it is amazingly small. Without conflicts around fraternities, it would almost be nonexistent.

Brown: In the "Social Change" piece you mention the "generation of faculty moving into deans' positions who came of age in the movements of the 60s." Does that describe your own journey? Did you become "disillusioned and professionalized" along the way? Did you "retool your professional obligations"? Could you tell me more about that journey?

Weinberg: I was born in 1965, so I am too young. My journey is probably more typical of the younger academics, who are becoming associate faculty and taking on administrative roles. I came into the academy because everybody was going to graduate school and I didn't want to go to law school. I was searching for a way to combine different passions: community organizing, writing, the world of ideas. I was also looking for a profession that would allow me to live my politics. I wanted an egalitarian marriage.

I was also driven into the academy by a passion for democracy. I wanted to spend my life working on ways to make communities (the places people live) more democratic. That is why I was attracted to community-based research and service learning. I wanted to raise my children in a social and political household. I probably would have left graduate school had community-based research and service learning not become acceptable ways of doing things. It gave me ways to combine my passions for community work with my love for writing and thinking. I stayed because I came to understand the untapped potential of universities. Along the way, I fell deeply in love with teaching.

Over time, I have become more optimistic and less professionalized. I see my work as a craft. I came very close to leaving the academy a few years ago. I had viewed myself as an academic who was focused externally. I had never envisioned myself as an administrator. I actually thought that I would be one of those people who moved back and forth between the nonprofit/government to university worlds. But, I became excited by academic administration. I came to work for a great college president, Rebecca Chopp.

Brown: In your "Social Change" piece, you say that "there is neither one magic factor nor even one linear process that leads to universities becoming an agent of social change." If so, does that mean that what is happening at Colgate cannot be replicated somewhere else?

Weinberg: The lessons learned can be replicated. I am a community organizer and educator, at heart. I don't think that there is a one-size-fits-all model. But, I do believe that we can train people with skills, concepts, and theories to build their own paths for their own communities.

Brown: And now…?

Weinberg: I am not sure! I am having fun. When an institution takes up public work/civic education as a driving principle you can achieve amazing results on students, faculty research, community development, alumni, and parents, and even helping to shape the agendas of foundations and trade associations. In my current role, I was able to advocate that civic learning become a top priority for Colgate. We are on the verge of universities becoming more relevant … or we could be.… I wanted to be part of that process. I also see management as another arena of public work. In three years, we have managed to deprofessionalize our student affairs division, recentering it around notions of public work. This is my own way of thinking about and contributing to a "democracy through the workplace" movement.

Having said that, I am ready for a new set of challenges. In January '06, I will be moving to World Learning to become the Senior Vice President for Academic Affairs and the provost of SIT —the School for International Training. I want to spend the next phase of my career working on civic education in more global settings. World Learning has been a leader in this field. They are also the only academic institution with a large international development operation. At any given point, they have about 3000 people working in over 100 countries on social and economic development projects. This position blends my dual passions for civic education and community development.

Brown: Thank you, Adam.

CHAPTER FOUR

Public Scholarship: The Perspective and a Story

Reconstructing a Democratic Tradition of Public Scholarship in the Land-Grant System

A Portrait of a University as a Young Citizen

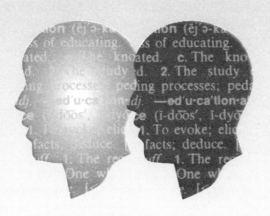

Reconstructing a Democratic Tradition of Public Scholarship in the Land-Grant System

Scott Peters

In her chapter in this book, Noëlle McAfee asks what kind of civic relationship there might be between the academy and the public. In this chapter, I explore the nature and promise of a civic relationship in which academic professionals take up and interweave both responsive expert and proactive social critic and change agent roles, including the little recognized role of acting, in McAfee's words, as "an ally in creating opportunities and ideas that support public making." For more than a century, many scholars in land-grant colleges of agriculture and human ecology (hereinafter "land-grant colleges") have taken up such roles by becoming engaged in public work that addresses not only the technical, but also the social, political, and cultural aspects of agricultural and environmental problems. In doing so, they have established one of the most important democratic traditions of public scholarship in American higher education.

The history and contemporary nature of this tradition are not widely known. Further, there is reason to believe that its future is seriously endangered. In relation to these problems, my own work as a scholar is centered on the threefold task of reconstructing it: first, by examining how and for what purposes scholars in land-grant colleges developed a democratic tradition of public scholarship; second, by identifying and interpreting the nature, meaning, and significance of the tradition in its historical and contemporary contexts; and third, by developing collaborative approaches to strengthening and defending it as one (among many) means of pursuing the "land-grant mission," a phrase that is often used to name the land-grant system's public purposes and work.

Drawing from what I am learning in my research, which is still in its exploratory stage, the story I tell in this chapter is both inspiring and troubling. While there was and still is a democratic tradition of public scholarship in land-grant colleges, it has been and continues to be obscured by the prevailing view of the land-grant mission as responsive, narrowly instrumental, and apolitical public service. Also, it has been and continues to be marginalized by technocratic tendencies and forces, and by the research university norm of civic detachment. Additionally, the story I tell illuminates the conflicting and conflicted nature of scholars' views about their political roles and stances, including how they should understand and work through what historian Thomas Bender has referred to as "the dilemma of the relation of expertise and democracy."[1]

History

The national land-grant system was established through the Morrill Acts of 1862 and 1890 and the Equity in Education Land-Grant Status Act of 1994. It consists of 105 institutions located in all 50 states and several U.S. territories. A unique structural feature of this system is its institutionalization in colleges of agriculture and human ecology of permanent mechanisms for engaging faculty, staff, and students as active participants in the world beyond the campus. These mechanisms are the national Agricultural Experiment Station System, which was established by the Hatch Act in 1887, and the national Cooperative Extension System, which was established by the Smith-Lever Act in 1914. Most of the annually recurring funding for these systems is provided by government sources. In the FY 2006 budget, the U.S. Department of Agriculture (USDA) provided more than $1 billion of funding, and an additional $1 billion or so was provided by state and county governments.[2]

---

[1] T. Bender, *Intellect and Public Life* (Baltimore, MD: Johns Hopkins University Press, 1993), 128.

[2] For the history of the land-grant system, see F. B. Mumford, *The Land Grant College Movement* (Columbia, MO: University of Missouri Agricultural Experiment Station, 1940); E. D. Ross, *Democracy's College: The Land-Grant Movement in the Formative Stage* (Ames, IA: The Iowa State College Press, 1942); E. D. Eddy, Jr., *Colleges for Our Land and Time: The Land-Grant Idea in American Education* (New York: Harper & Brothers, 1957); and National Association of State Universities and Land-Grant Colleges (NASULGC), *The Land-Grant Tradition* (Washington, DC: NASULGC, 1995.) Budget figures are taken from http://www.csrees.usda.gov/about/offices/budget.html. (Accessed October 16, 2007.)

The story of the origins and development of a democratic tradition of public scholarship during the early history of land-grant colleges and their affiliated experiment station and extension systems has never been told. It has been obscured (in part) by the prevailing view of the historical nature and significance of the land-grant mission. The prevailing view in academic literatures, official institutional rhetoric, and informal culture characterizes the land-grant mission (in both historical and contemporary contexts) as "public service." It positions the land-grant system as *the* historical exemplar of the so-called "service ideal" in American higher education.[3]

> *"Public science, as we envision it, is a form of public scholarship."*
>
> ("Toward a Public Science: Building a New Social Contract between Science and Society," *HEX*, 1999.)

As it is reproduced in academic literatures, official institutional rhetoric, and informal culture, there are four main problems with the prevailing view of the historical nature and significance of the land-grant mission:

- First, *it is entirely responsive and one-directional.* It characterizes the land-grant system's engagement with the world beyond the campus as consisting only of one-way transfers and applications of technical knowledge and expertise that are made in response to the demands for help by external clients and constituencies.

- Second, *it is too narrow and instrumental.* It casts the history of the land-grant system's public purposes and work as being about only technical, material, and economic matters.

---

[3] For a comprehensive review of the way academic public service has been conceptualized and pursued in American history, see P. Crosson, *Public Service in Higher Education: Practices and Priorities* (Washington, DC: Association for the Study of Higher Education, 1983). In her book, Crosson writes that the land-grant system provides the "most celebrated and successful example of the articulation and fulfillment of the service ideal" (p. 22). For a rare philosophical discussion of the land-grant mission, see J. T. Bonnen, "The Land-Grant Idea and the Evolving Outreach University," in *University-Community Collaborations for the Twenty-First Century: Outreach Scholarship for Youth and Families*, eds. R. M. Lerner and L. K. Simon (New York: Garland Publishing, Inc., 1998).

- Third, *it is embarrassingly self-congratulatory*. It implies that the history of the pursuit of the land-grant mission is one of complete, continuous, and unambiguous success.

- Finally—and for me, most important—*it is apolitical*. Instead of using a political language of public relationships and work involving people with different types and levels of interests, knowledge, expertise, and power, the prevailing view employs a mechanical language of responsive public service that focuses on the provision of technical solutions to technical problems through instrumental transactions between active and allegedly "unbiased" experts and passive, needy clients. Such a language obscures the politics of scholars' engagement in the world beyond the campus. It also reinforces the self-congratulatory story line about land-grant history.[4]

To illuminate and reconstruct a democratic tradition of public scholarship in the early history of land-grant colleges, we need to do two things. First, we need to position the story of the origins and development of land-grant colleges within the context of the larger story of the academic revolution of the late 19th and early 20th centuries. Second, we need to adopt a different conception of the historical nature and significance of the land-grant mission. Instead of viewing this mission as public service, we need to view it

---

[4] My characterization of the prevailing view of the historical nature and significance of the land-grant mission is not a so-called "straw man." It is consistently reproduced in academic literatures. See, for example, Mumford, *The Land Grant College Movement*; Ross, *Democracy's College: The Land-Grant Movement in the Formative Stage*; Eddy, Jr., *Colleges for Our Land and Time: The Land-Grant Idea in American Education*; A. Nevins, *The State Universities and Democracy* (Urbana, IL: University of Illinois Press, 1962); J. B. Edmond, *The Magnificent Charter: The Origin and Role of the Morrill Land-Grant Colleges and Universities* (Hicksville, NY: Exposition Press, 1978); W. D. Rasmussen, *Taking the University to the People: Seventy-Five Years of Cooperative Extension* (Ames, IA: Iowa State University Press, 1989); J. R. Campbell, *Reclaiming a Lost Heritage: Land-Grant and Other Higher Education Initiatives for the Twenty-First Century* (Ames, IA: Iowa State University Press, 1995); National Research Council, *Colleges of Agriculture at the Land-Grant Universities: Public Service and Public Policy* (Washington, DC: National Academy Press, 1996); Kellogg Commission on the Future of State and Land-Grant Institutions, *Returning to Our Roots: The Engaged Institution* (Washington, DC: National Association of State Universities and Land-Grant Colleges, 1999); and K. Ward, *Faculty Service Roles and the Scholarship of Engagement* (San Francisco, CA: Jossey-Bass, 2003).

as public work: work that Harry Boyte defines as "sustained effort by a mix of people who solve public problems or create goods, material or cultural, of general benefit."[5]

The academic revolution included the emergence of the research university and the accompanying process of professionalizing the academic calling. According to Richard Hofstadter, during the academic revolution scholars began to overcome their "traditional civic passivity and take an active part in the shaping of political events." Armed with "empirical specialized skills," Hofstadter writes, scholars had "not only prestige but some real marketable advice to bring to public life." For the first time, "the profession developed the capacity both for large-scale innovative work in scholarship and for social criticism and practical contribution to the political dialogue of American society."[6]

In exercising the capacity to take up the academic profession's expert and social critic roles, scholars encountered an important dilemma: how and for what purposes they should relate their expertise to the process and work of democracy. While engaging in democracy offered potential benefits, it also carried potential risks. For example, if we take democracy to mean rule by the people, or "self-rule," as historian Robert Wiebe puts it, there was (and of course still is) a risk of becoming engaged in it in technocratic ways that disempower, sideline, or marginalize citizens.[7]

The history of how scholars have perceived and worked through the dilemma of the relation of expertise and democracy (or failed to do so) is highly complex and many sided, conditioned by situation, context, discipline, institutional type, and many other matters. Despite this complexity, it is possible to identify three different perspectives on the dilemma, tied to three positions in the

---

[5] H. C. Boyte, *Everyday Politics: Reconnecting Citizens and Public Life* (Philadelphia, PA: University of Pennsylvania Press, 2004), 5.

[6] R. Hofstadter, "The Revolution in Higher Education," in *Paths of American Thought*, (eds.) A. M. Schlesinger, Jr. and M. White (Boston: Houghton Mifflin Company, 1963), 287-288.

[7] See R. H. Wiebe, *Self-Rule: A Cultural History of American Democracy* (Chicago: University of Chicago Press, 1995).

debate that emerged during the late 19th and early 20th centuries about the "proper" role of scholars in civic life.

The first position is that the proper role of scholars in civic life is, effectively, no role at all. Abraham Flexner wrote the classic statement in support of this position in his 1930 book, *Universities: American, English, German*. In it, he argues that the "university must shelter and develop thinkers, experimenters, inventors, teachers, and students, who, without responsibility for action, will explore the phenomena of social life and endeavor to understand them." While scholars could, as he put it, "maintain contacts with the actual world," they were to be held "irresponsible" for addressing the problems of the world as well as "indifferent to the effect and use" of the knowledge and theory they produce.[8]

Walter Lippmann embraced Flexner's position in "The Scholar in a Troubled World." In this address, delivered in 1932 during the Great Depression, Lippmann described scholars as being torn between two different consciences: a "civic conscience" that tells a scholar that he or she "ought to be doing something about the world's troubles," and the "conscience of the scholar, which tells him [*sic*] that as one whose business it is to examine the nature of things, to imagine how they work, and to test continually the proposals of his imagination, he must preserve a quiet indifference to the immediate." By "the immediate," Lippmann was referring to the messy, contentious world of civic life. The main point of his speech was to argue in favor of *detachment* from civic life as the right and proper stance of the scholar. As he put it, "I doubt whether the student can do a greater work for his nation in this grave moment of its history than to detach himself from its preoccupations, refusing to let himself be absorbed by distractions about which, as a scholar, he can do almost nothing."[9]

The second position in the debate, held by what Mark C. Smith calls "service intellectuals," is that scholars should reject calls for civic detachment and irresponsibility by becoming actively engaged in civic

---

[8] A. Flexner, *Universities: American, English, German* (New York: Oxford University Press, 1930), 10, 15.

[9] W. Lippmann, "The Scholar in a Troubled World," in *The Essential Lippmann: A Political Philosophy for Liberal Democracy*, (eds.) C. Rossiter and J. Lare (New York: Random House, 1963), 509-510, 515.

life. But in doing so, they must restrict their role to that of the responsive expert who provides technical assistance and scientific knowledge from a stance of disinterested neutrality. Service intellectuals are supposed to follow the principle of "experts on tap, not on top." In effect, they work through the dilemma of the relation of expertise and democracy by placing themselves *outside* of politics, including both the formal partisan politics of government policymaking and the informal and less partisan politics that Boyte refers to as "everyday politics." In ideal terms, service intellectuals are to have no political identity or agency of their own. In other words, in their professional work as scholars they are not to function as citizens, but rather as servants of citizens.[10]

The third position, held by what Smith calls "purposivists," is that scholars should not be restricted to merely being "on tap," nor should they be restricted to a responsive stance of disinterested neutrality. Instead, they should be allowed—even encouraged—to exercise their political agency by taking up a *proactive* stance that is both interested and nonneutral. While they might function at times as responsive experts in the service-intellectual mode, they may also function as proactive critics and change agents. In taking up these roles, they not only make critical judgments about social problems, they also take action to address them in ways that openly side with particular ideals, interests, ends, and values. By placing themselves *inside* rather than outside of the work of politics, purposivists integrate their professional and civic identities. How they perceive and work through the dilemma of the relation of expertise and democracy will vary, depending on the realities and dynamics of specific contexts and situations, and their political views and values (including their view of the nature and meaning of democracy).

Utilizing Smith's theoretical distinction between service intellectuals and purposivists as tools in my study of land-grant history, I have

---

[10] See M. C. Smith, *Social Science in the Crucible: The American Debate Over Objectivity and Purpose, 1918-1941* (Durham, NC: Duke University Press, 1994). Smith attributes the "experts on tap, not on top" phrase to Charles Merriam, a political scientist from the University of Chicago whom Smith characterizes as a service intellectual (p. 105). For classic statements of the service-intellectual role and stance, see T. V. Smith and L. D. White, (eds.), *Chicago: An Experiment in Social Research* (Chicago: University of Chicago Press, 1929); G. A. Lundberg, *Can Science Save Us?* (New York: David McKay Company, Inc., 1961); and M. Hammersley, *The Politics of Social Research* (Thousand Oaks, CA: Sage Publications, 1995).

learned that many scholars who worked in and through land-grant colleges and their affiliated experiment station and extension systems positioned themselves in their writings and speeches either as responsive service intellectuals or as detached and "irresponsible" scholars of the variety Flexner and Lippmann endorsed. But many also positioned themselves as proactive and deeply political purposivists. They did so as public intellectuals who spoke *to* public audiences in critical ways about public issues and problems, and/or as public scholars who worked *with* specific, localized publics in public work initiatives. In doing so, they positioned themselves as a nonneutral means of transformation in direct relation to a pressing problem: the erosion and "exhaustion" of the soil.[11]

As historian Stephen Stoll has shown, the problem of soil erosion and exhaustion was a *social* rather than merely a technical problem. It was economic, moral, cultural, and political in both its nature and its consequences. In relation to this social problem, and numerous others (e.g., problems related to nutrition and health, youth development, poverty, and rural government and culture), faculty and

---

[11] While Smith examines only social scientists in his work, his theoretical distinction between service intellectuals and purposivists can be posed and applied well beyond the social sciences to include every academic discipline and field. In my view, public scholarship is distinctly different from the more familiar "public intellectual" tradition in American higher education. Public intellectuals are typically defined by their engagement in the work of social criticism through scholarship that examines and analyzes public issues for general public audiences. See R. Jacoby, *The Last Intellectuals: American Culture in the Age of Academe* (New York: The Noonday Press, 1987); E. Said, *Representations of the Intellectual* (New York: Vintage Books, 1994); L. Fink, *Progressive Intellectuals and the Dilemmas of Democratic Commitment* (Cambridge, MA: Harvard University Press, 1997); M. Walzer, *The Company of Critics: Social Criticism and Political Commitment in the Twentieth Century* (New York: Basic Books, 2002); and A. M. Melzzer, J. Weinberger, and M. R. Zinman, eds., *The Public Intellectual: Between Philosophy and Politics* (Lanham, MD: Rowman & Littlefield, 2003). The defining characteristic of public scholarship is not social criticism that is delivered to general public audiences, but rather personal, face-to-face engagement in localized public work. In my view, public scholars engage in scholarly work that is conducted to some significant degree both in public and with particular publics. They combine the work of scholarship with the work of politics. By politics, I refer to the means by which individuals and groups develop and exercise power in a wide variety of settings as they seek to identify, deliberate upon, negotiate, and take action to advance their self-interests, their common interests, and larger public interests.

community-based extension educators in the land-grant system positioned themselves as both responsive experts and proactive social critics and change agents. In taking up the latter, they sought not only to inform decision making, but also to change the behaviors, attitudes, values, and ideals of their rural constituencies.[12]

Contrary to the prevailing view of the historical nature and significance of the land-grant mission, the public purposes and work of many scholars who were employed by land-grant colleges of agriculture during the late 19th and early 20th centuries were not limited to responsive technical problem solving. They also included the proactive pursuit of what Liberty Hyde Bailey referred to in 1897 as a "self-sustaining" agriculture. Bailey was a horticultural scientist who served as dean of Cornell University's College of Agriculture from 1903 to 1913. Committed to what Stoll has referred to as an "ethic of permanence," Bailey viewed the pursuit of a self-sustaining agriculture as a multidimensional project that had technical, scientific, moral, cultural, political, and even spiritual dimensions. In his view, such a project would both require and result in the development of a new rural civilization "worthy of the best American ideals." "We are now beginning to be consciously concerned in the development of a thoroughly good and sound rural civilization," he announced in 1909. "The colleges of agriculture will be the most important agencies in this evolution."[13]

---

[12] See S. Stoll, *Larding the Lean Earth: Soil and Society in Nineteenth-Century America* (New York: Hill and Wang, 2002).

[13] L. H. Bailey, *The Principles of Fruit Growing* (New York, NY: Macmillan, 1897), 26. S. Stoll, *Larding the Lean Earth: Soil and Society in Nineteenth-Century America*, 19-31. L. H. Bailey, *The College of Agriculture and the State* (Ithaca, NY: New York State College of Agriculture, 1909), 1. L. H. Bailey, "The Better Preparation of Men for College and Station Work," in *Proceedings of the Twenty-Third Annual Convention of the Association of American Agricultural Colleges and Experiment Stations*, eds. A. C. True and W. H. Beal (Washington, DC: Government Printing Office, 1910), 25-26. For more about Bailey's work and views on these matters, see S. J. Peters and P. A. Morgan, "The Country Life Commission: Reconsidering a Milestone in American Agricultural History," *Agricultural History*, Vol. 78, No. 3 (Summer 2004): 289-316; S. J. Peters, "Every Farmer Should Be Awakened: Liberty Hyde Bailey's Vision of Agricultural Extension Work," *Agricultural History*, Vol. 80, No. 2 (Spring 2006): 190-219; and P. A. Morgan and S. J. Peters, "The Foundations of Planetary Agrarianism: Thomas Berry and Liberty Hyde Bailey," *Journal of Agricultural and Environmental Ethics*, Vol. 19, No. 5 (August 2006): 443-468.

Bailey argued in 1907 that land-grant colleges "contribute to the public welfare in a very broad way, extending their influence far beyond the technique of agricultural trades." Elaborating on this theme in 1909, he proclaimed: "While the College of Agriculture is concerned directly with increasing the producing power of land, its activities cannot be limited narrowly to this field. It must stand broadly for rural civilization."[14]

Bailey's broad, highly ambitious, and inherently political vision of the public purposes and work of land-grant colleges was not a momentary anomaly. It was incorporated into the rhetoric and culture of the national cooperative extension system. This can be seen in the opening paragraph of a book published in 1930, entitled *The Cooperative Extension System*, authored by two national extension leaders:

> There is a new leaven at work in rural America. It is stimulating to better endeavor in farming and home making, bringing rural people together in groups for social intercourse and study, solving community and neighborhood problems, fostering better relations and common endeavor between town and country, bringing recreation, debate, pageantry, the drama and art into the rural community, developing cooperation and enriching the life and broadening the vision of rural men and women. This new leaven is the cooperative extension work of the state agricultural colleges and the federal Department of Agriculture, which is being carried on in cooperation with the counties and rural people throughout the United States.[15]

In this remarkable paragraph, we catch a glimpse of how at least some of the scholars who had a hand in developing and institutionalizing the agricultural extension work of the land-grant system would have answered McAfee's question about the kind

---

[14] L. H. Bailey, "The Outlook for the College of Agriculture," in *Addresses at the Dedication of the Buildings of the New York State College of Agriculture* (Ithaca, NY: Cornell University, 1907), 40. Bailey, *The College of Agriculture and the State*, 11.

[15] C. B. Smith and M. C. Wilson, *The Agricultural Extension System of the United States* (New York, NY: John Wiley & Sons, 1930), 1.

of civic relationship there might be between the academy and the public. With the use of the intriguing metaphor of a "leaven," we see a relationship that involved a transformative and proactive organizing role for the state (i.e., land-grant) agricultural colleges. We see a relationship that included the work of building publics that debate, solve, and pursue a broad, multidimensional array of technical, social, economic, civic, and cultural problems and ideals. In essence, we see a relationship that reflects an embrace of the task that Liberty Hyde Bailey had assigned to land-grant colleges of agriculture in 1909: "to direct and to aid in developing the entire rural civilization." As Bailey noted, such a task placed these colleges "within the realm of statesmanship." In other words, it placed them within the realm of *politics*. It is within this realm that academic professionals in the land-grant system became engaged in public work as public scholars. In doing so, they took up both responsive expert and proactive social critic and change agent roles, acting not only as participants in but also as organizers of public work, and as allies in creating opportunities and ideas that support public making.[16]

There are no published histories of the origins and early development of the tradition of public scholarship in the agricultural colleges of the land-grant system. This does not mean that we do not know anything about the political nature of the land-grant system's agricultural work during its formative years. Scholars in the field of agricultural history have helped us to see that academic professionals who sought to address agricultural problems and issues often did so by practicing an oppressive technocratic politics aimed at forcing the industrialization of agriculture. Their technocratic work effectively—but not necessarily intentionally—advanced a national "cheap food" policy that privileged urban and corporate interests and national economic aims. It not only impoverished and disempowered farmers, women,

---

[16] Bailey, *The College of Agriculture and the State*, 12.

and rural communities, but it also wracked serious cultural and environmental damage.[17]

> "Community members were often skeptical of professional research findings, for the good reason that they often did not reflect local experience."
>
> ("Public Scholarship and the Land-Grant Idea," *HEX*, 1997.)

While the historical tradition of public scholarship in the agricultural experiment station and extension work of the land-grant system included practitioners who sought to "direct and aid" in the task of developing a new rural civilization through an oppressive technocratic politics, it also included practitioners who took up this task through productive, developmental, participatory, and democratic varieties of civic republican and populist politics. For those who embraced a democratic rather than technocratic politics—including Liberty Hyde Bailey, Kenyon Butterfield, Mary Mims, and many others—the task was not to develop a rural civilization that would fuel an industrial economy with cheap food. Nor was it restricted to the de-

---

[17] For the oppressive technocratic story about the land-grant system, see J. Hightower, *Hard Tomatoes, Hard Times* (Cambridge, MA: Schenkman Publishing Company, 1973-1978); C. E. Rosenberg, *No Other Gods: On Science and American Social Thought* (Baltimore, MD: The Johns Hopkins University Press, 1976/1997); W. Berry, *The Unsettling of America: Culture and Agriculture*, 3rd edition (San Francisco, CA: Sierra Club Books, 1977/1996); D. D. Danbom, *The Resisted Revolution: Urban America and the Industrialization of Agriculture, 1900-1930* (Ames, IA: Iowa State University Press, 1979); A. I. Marcus, *Agricultural Science and the Quest for Legitimacy: Farmers, Agricultural Colleges, and Experiment Stations, 1870-1890* (Ames, IA: Iowa State University Press, 1985); K. Jellison, *Entitled to Power: Farm Women and Technology, 1913-1963* (Chapel Hill, NC: The University of North Carolina Press, 1993); M. Neth, *Preserving the Family Farm: Women, Community, and the Foundations of Agribusiness in the Midwest, 1900-1940* (Baltimore, MD: The Johns Hopkins University Press, 1995); H. S. Barron, *Mixed Harvest: The Second Great Transformation in the Rural North, 1870-1930* (Chapel Hill, NC: The University of North Carolina Press, 1997); R. R. Kline, *Consumers in the Country: Technology and Social Change in Rural America* (Baltimore, MD: The Johns Hopkins University Press, 2000); and D. Fitzgerald, *Every Farm a Factory: The Industrial Ideal in American Agriculture* (New Haven, CT: Yale University Press, 2003).

velopment of a rural civilization that raised farmers' material and economic well-being. Rather, as Liberty Hyde Bailey put it, the task was to develop a rural civilization "worthy of the best American ideals." Such a civilization would certainly be worthy of the ideal of material and economic well-being for all. But it would also be worthy of the democratic ideal and practice of self-rule, through which the common people, functioning as citizens, work as stewards of the environment, and as cooperative producers not only of the commonwealth, but also of the culture and politics of their neighborhoods and communities. It is the tradition of public scholarship in the land-grant system that embraced and pursued this ideal that I am seeking to reconstruct in and through my historical research.[18]

Contemporary Practice

The possibilities and promise of the democratic tradition of public scholarship in land-grant colleges have never been fully realized. The tradition has been increasingly marginalized over the years by technocratic tendencies and forces, and by the power and influence of the research university norm of civic detachment. Even so, it has survived into the present. But in my judgment, its continuing survival into the future appears increasingly unlikely. This lends considerable urgency to the task of reconstructing it.

---

[18] Works by some of the more democratic-minded figures in the history of the agricultural work of the land-grant system include L. H. Bailey, *The Holy Earth* (New York: Charles Scribner's Sons, 1915); K. L. Butterfield, *The Farmer and the New Day* (New York: MacMillan, 1920); A. G. Arvold, *The Little Country Theater*, (New York: MacMillan, 1922); M. Mims, *The Awakening Community* (New York: MacMillan, 1932); M. Patten, *The Arts Workshop of Rural America: A Study of the Rural Arts Program of the Agricultural Extension System* (New York: Columbia University Press, 1937); and R. Gard, *Grassroots Theater: A Search for Regional Arts in America* (Madison, WI: University of Wisconsin Press, 1955). As the latter of these works suggest, the democratic tradition included a strong cultural dimension that utilized the arts as a means of civic development. For a brief account of this dimension and a fuller treatment of the conflicting narratives about the land-grant mission, see S. J. Peters, *Changing the Story about Higher Education's Public Purposes and Work: Land-Grants, Liberty, and the Little Country Theater* (Ann Arbor, MI: Imagining America, 2007).

Here, I want to stress the meaning and purpose of reconstruction that William Sullivan speaks of in his ongoing study of the civic identity and practices of the professions. The aim of reconstruction, Sullivan writes, is "both to better understand the intrinsic purposes of the professional enterprise and to suggest the lines along which the enterprise needs to move if it is to reclaim those purposes more vigorously and coherently." According to him, the central intrinsic purposes of the professional enterprise are expressed through a pledge professionals have historically made to "deploy their technical expertise and judgment not only skillfully but for public-regarding ends and in a public-regarding way." The problem, as Sullivan and others see it, is that a conception of professionalism that stresses public ends and practices—a conception that Sullivan refers to as "civic professionalism"—has been eclipsed by a conception that stresses private economic and instrumental ends and practices. Given this problem, Sullivan writes, it is "far from clear" whether professionals in a variety of fields "will be able to sustain their social importance without re-engaging the public over the value of their work to the society at large." If the professions are to have a future, he goes on to say, "they may need to rest their case on the basis of a civic rather than a wholly technical understanding of what it is that professionals are about."[19]

Sullivan's view of what the professions in general may need to do to sustain their social importance into the future holds a great deal of relevance for the specific case of the academic profession. It is especially relevant for scholars who work in land-grant colleges. In my research, I have found that a civic conception of academic professionalism that stresses public ends and practices is still embraced

---

[19] W. M. Sullivan, *Work and Integrity: The Crisis and Promise of Professionalism in America* (San Francisco, CA: Jossey-Bass, 2005), 180. W. M. Sullivan, "Engaging the Civic Option: A New Academic Professionalism?" *Campus Compact Reader* (Summer 2003), 10. W. M. Sullivan, "What Is Left of Professionalism After Managed Care?" *Hastings Center Report*, Vol. 29, No. 2 (1999): 6. Recent studies of the history of the professions in American society tell a similar story. For example, see the account of the erosion of "social trustee professionalism" and the rise of "expert professionalism" in S. Brint, *In an Age of Experts: The Changing Role of Professionals in Politics and Public Life* (Princeton, NJ: Princeton University Press, 1994).

by some of the scholars who are employed by these colleges. But in my (and sometimes their) judgment, it is increasingly at odds with and threatened by a growing privatized conception that not only privileges the economic value of technical expertise and accomplishment, but also normatively positions scholars outside of civic life. In this context, scholars who wish to position themselves inside civic life as democratic-minded public scholars will have to get both the public and their own academic peers and administrators to understand and support not only "the value of their work to the society at large," but also the value of their work to their academic disciplines and institutions.

> *"To see land grant education not as a neutral service but as public work is to see it in light of its best tradition."*
>
> ("The Civic Mission Question in Land Grant Education," *HEX*, 2001.)

To put it mildly, this is a tall order. In a deliberate attempt to contribute to its pursuit, my research aims to identify and interpret the nature, purpose, meaning, and significance of the contemporary practice of public scholarship in land-grant colleges. In the exploratory stage of this research, several colleagues and I have conducted both individual and focus group interviews with more than 60 scholars from 10 different land-grant universities who were identified by their peers as being exemplars of public engagement in their home states. In our individual interviews, we drew out detailed, firsthand stories of scholars' practices and experiences as direct, face-to-face participants in public work at the local community level.

In both the individual and focus group interviews we have conducted, faculty told more than 75 practice stories. Some of their stories are brief accounts of single events or short-term projects. Others are lengthy, elaborately detailed descriptions of long-term initiatives that unfolded over many months, sometimes even many years. In these stories, faculty spoke of why and how they developed close, working relationships with particular individuals, groups, and organizations, including small- and large-scale farmers and their associations (e.g., vegetable growers, grape or apple growers, and dairy farmers), golf course managers, government agencies, legislators and elected officials, nongovernment organizations (NGOs), and community organizations and institutions.

Most of the practice stories faculty members told focus on social problems related to the environment. These include environmental pollution and human health problems caused (or thought to be caused) by farming practices, or by the use of chemicals to control weeds and pests by businesses, homeowners, and golf course and park managers. Some stories focus on work related to public policy debates, such as whether genetically modified organisms (GMOs) should be promoted, adopted, regulated, or banned, what to do about an overpopulation of deer in residential areas, and a number of other wildlife and natural resource management problems. Other stories involve community disputes related to migrant labor, racial, ethnic, and class issues, zoning and land-use planning, and urban sprawl. Still others focus on problems associated with poverty, economic decline, population loss, the loss of a sense of community, youth violence and substance abuse, and public policies related to student achievement in rural and small-town schools.

By way of illustration, consider the work of a professor whom I interviewed from the natural science discipline of horticulture. The focus of this faculty member's academic work is problems related to growing berry crops. Berry growers face different problems, depending on which crop they grow. For example, strawberry growers face serious challenges in managing weeds, birds are a special problem for blueberry growers, and soil diseases cause problems for raspberry growers. As I learned from conducting three separate interviews with him, in helping growers address such problems, he takes on a responsive expert role as a scientist. However, as I also learned, he intentionally takes on a proactive change-agent role as a critic and educator as well.

We see this in a practice story he told me about his role in addressing a deeply controversial social problem related to the development and use of GMOs in strawberry production. A particular chemical company has developed a powerful herbicide. It can

only be used with specific crops: that is, crops that have been genetically engineered to be compatible with the herbicide. To help them
combat weeds, strawberry growers are calling for the development
of herbicide compatible strawberries. The problem, this faculty
member told me, is that "there are a lot of issues about [these]
strawberries that most growers don't think about," including consumer acceptance and the effects on the environment. In relation to
this problem, he gave a talk on the advantages and disadvantages of
herbicide compatible strawberries at the annual meeting for his
state's berry-growers' association. After he gave his talk, he handed
out a survey asking growers' for their views about the issues he had
raised. He then shared the results of the survey with the association's
members.

Speaking of his role in this story, the faculty member told me:
"I was intentionally not being biased. I gave the advantages and
said what some of the concerns are." According to the results of
his survey, his talk changed growers' minds. The last question on
the survey asked whether growers would use herbicide compatible
strawberries if they were available today. Most of them answered no,
even though just a few months earlier their association had taken
a public position strongly in favor of the development and use of
GMO technologies, including herbicide compatible strawberries.
While few growers said on the survey that they would never use
GMOs, most now reported some uncertainty about whether they
should use them. Importantly, their uncertainty was not solely
about the technical and economic aspects of strawberry production. As this faculty member noted, "a lot of it had to do not with the
biology, but with the marketing and the social and environmental
implications that they hadn't thought of."

In reflecting on the meaning of his story, the faculty member
told me the following:

> Some people take the position that the desires and the
> needs of the growers, the producers, trump everything
> else. If they say, "We want [herbicide compatible]
> strawberries," we give it to them. But I contrast that
> with other people who may have different views of
> what the land-grant university should do. My ap-

proach would be to see if we can't balance these in
some way.

"Balancing" different views of what the land-grant university
should do has implications for how this faculty member views his
roles and work with growers. As he puts it:

> I see my role as trying to identify some key areas of re-
> search that I can work in that will not only help growers
> with some immediate problems, but maybe push their
> thinking a little bit in terms of issues that might involve
> sustainability, and get them thinking a little bit broader
> than how they thought in the past. I do this because I
> feel not only a commitment to them, but a commitment
> to society, to people who pay my salary, to [this state's]
> residents. My work should not be focused exclusively
> on the grower community. I have an obligation to the
> greater part of society, too, and if I can help growers
> produce high quality fruit in a way that is more envi-
> ronmentally sustainable, everybody wins.

In considering this little practice story, we gain important insight
into why and how a scholar from a natural science discipline views
his work with growers in a way that compels him to take on both
responsive expert and proactive critic and change-agent roles. The
story also reveals the conflicted nature of his views about his political
stance. While he positions himself as being "unbiased," when he tells
us that he seeks to "push" growers thinking, we see that he has what
amounts to a bias. We see that he is neither impartial nor neutral.
He is partial to and nonneutral about environmental sustainability.
To pursue his commitment to sustainability, he moves beyond the disinterested expert role of imparting scientific knowledge by taking up
a role as a purposive educator aimed at changing growers' social and
environmental consciousness. In his educator role, he seeks to teach
growers to think not just of what they could do to address technical
problems related to growing strawberries (namely, use herbicide
compatible strawberries), but also what they should do, given the
potential environmental, economic, and social risks and implications
of a new technology. The reason he does this, he tells us, is because
he has an obligation to work not only for the interests of growers, but
also for "the greater society," including "people who pay my salary."

To borrow from William Sullivan's work, in reading this scholar's practice story we come to see one of the ways that public scholars in land-grant colleges of agriculture enact the pledge civic professionals make to "deploy their technical expertise and judgment not only skillfully but for public-regarding ends and in a public-regarding way." And in seeing this, we gain a civic rather than wholly technical understanding of what at least some of the scholars who are employed by land-grant colleges of agriculture are about.

In analyzing and interpreting the full set of practice stories my colleagues and I have constructed with our research participants, I am finding three recurring patterns that seem especially interesting and important:

1. *Many of the scholars we interviewed hold a highly interactive view of the land-grant mission that both authorizes and compels them to engage as proactive participants in public work.*

2. *Many of the scholars we interviewed say that they strive to work on behalf of their personal views of the public good or interest rather than the self-interests of individuals or the common interests of particular groups. In doing so, they often position themselves as being "unbiased" or "neutral," working from a political stance that many of them refer to as the "middle."*

3. *Many of the scholars we interviewed claim that the kind of public engagement they value and pursue as academic professionals is not valued, supported, or pursued by most of their academic peers. Not surprisingly, many also express deeply pessimistic views about the future.*

I briefly discuss each of these patterns below.

The Land-Grant Mission

In the previous section of this chapter I argued that the prevailing view of the land-grant mission is responsive, narrowly instrumental, and apolitical public service. With respect to McAfee's question about the kind of civic relationship there might be between the academy and the public, such a view suggests a thin relationship that does not include acting as "an ally in creating opportunities and ideas that support public making." But most of the scholars we have interviewed in our research do not accept the prevailing view.[20]

Consider the following view of the land-grant mission that was articulated by a professor in the natural science discipline of plant breeding:

> I would argue that the mission of the land-grant is interaction with the people in the state. If we want to contribute to the collective wisdom—and that includes us as everyone else around the state—then I think it means interacting with people, wrestling with people to understand the issues that are being confronted and figure out what our piece in that picture is. What can we do to contribute to greater understanding or better dialogue or public policy that really will help address them? As a college that focuses on food, food science, agricultural areas, environmental areas, that sort of revolve around that, I think our piece of this is about sustainable landscape design and management, and thinking about how are the landscapes—urban, semi-urban and rural—in the state used, and how can we make that something that is more sustainable, in the most honest sense of that word. That's what I think of as the land-grant mission for our college, particularly given the kinds of disciplines that we represent.

This view positions land-grant faculty as proactive participants in public work: not as volunteers, but as scholars. It both compels and authorizes scholars to establish reciprocal relationships between the university and the public that hold both democratic and academic promise. At their best, such relationships are not only civic or political in nature, in the sense that they involve deliberation and action about public issues. They are also scholarly, in the sense that they serve as a crucial means of informing, shaping, and sometimes even conducting a scholar's research.

---

[20] With respect to the role of serving as an ally in public making work, it is important to note that there is a significant difference between providing ideas and providing opportunities. The former can be done indirectly and at a distance, without ever coming into relationship with a public. The latter is inherently direct and face-to-face. The opportunities that support public making that land-grant colleges of agriculture and human ecology provide through their institutionalized extension and experiment station systems are a large part of what makes these colleges distinctive.

One point needs to be stressed with regard to this first recurring pattern in our interview data. We see it in the following comments made in an interview with another professor in a natural science discipline. This scholar said that for her, the "land-grant mission has to do with sustaining communities, making sure knowledge that gets generated builds and strengthens communities and doesn't jeopardize them." But she was quick to add the following: "This view of the land-grant mission is a minority view in my department. The majority view is that we're here to advance knowledge, we're here to advance our discipline, we're here to educate students." Not only this scholar, but many of the scholars we interviewed who articulated highly interactive views of the land-grant mission that attend to civic as well as technical problems and issues also claimed that such a view is not the norm in their academic departments and institutions. What we should learn from this is that scholars who hold highly interactive views of the land-grant mission are not only up against the prevailing apolitical public service view of that mission, but also the research university norm of civic detachment. When these are combined, as I think they often are, it places public scholars in an exceedingly difficult position. Efforts to reconstruct a democratic tradition of public scholarship in land-grant colleges must take this situation into account.

Working for the Public Good from the "Middle"

In a focus group interview that I conducted with a diverse group of 15 faculty members from a variety of disciplines, I asked them who they think they work for. Here is how a professor in the natural science discipline of entomology answered my question:

> I've started thinking recently, who are my clients? We have an onion industry in [this state] that's worth about $50 million or so, and these people, I don't know if it's the sulfur in the onions or what, but they have told faculty members, "You work for us. You work for the onion industry." A number of different commodities somewhat have that attitude. But when I think about who I work for—and I think this is part of how I started to feel comfortable with the land-grant mission—I

work for the people of [this state], and I work through some growers to achieve an end. And the end would be things like environmental quality and pest management. It would be supporting an agricultural community, because I think it adds to the landscape and to the quality of life in the state. All of these things, I work through growers to obtain. But my clients are really the people of [this state], not necessarily the onion or cabbage growers, for example. I mean, I don't like to look at it that I'm working just for the cabbage growers. I work for the public good as I see it.

In this answer, we are provided with a provocative image of a faculty member resisting the claims of special agricultural interests that he is supposed to work for them, insisting instead that he works "for the public good as I see it." He implies that the land-grant mission provides an, if not *the*, authority for his view of whom he should work for. I find a similar pattern of speaking among many of the scholars we interviewed.

There are two things about this pattern that should be noted. First, it rarely conjures up images of publics engaged in deliberation about what should be done to advance the public good or interest. Rather, it conjures up images of individual scholars making judgments about the public good or interest on their own. As the above scholar said, "I work for the public good *as I see it*." Such a statement may seem quite praiseworthy. But from the perspective of how judgments about the public good are best made, it is actually quite troubling. By definition, the public good cannot be determined by scholars on their own. It can only be determined by the work of deliberating publics.

Despite the deeply interactive and relational view of the land-grant mission, which many public scholars espouse, the pattern of individualizing judgments about the public good suggests to me that the contemporary version of the tradition of public scholarship in land-grant colleges is not sufficiently interactive, relational, democratic, or public. To know what the public good is and how to work for it, public scholars need to engage in deliberation with their fellow citizens beyond the academy. It is not clear whether or to what extent they do so.

The second thing to note about this pattern has to do with the conflicted and conflicting claims scholars make about their political roles and stances. In positioning themselves as working on behalf of their personal view of the public good, many of the scholars we interviewed also position themselves as being "unbiased" or "neutral," working from a political stance that many of them refer to as the "middle." For example, in one of our focus group interviews that was devoted to a discussion of the practice story about herbicide compatible strawberries, which I quoted earlier, an associate professor in a social science discipline said that he is "very sympathetic" to the role he sees the natural scientist playing in the practice story. "This is the kind of work we all do: trying to bring knowledge to bear, looking at the question from all sides, not taking—not advocating a particular point of view." But as he continued, he suggested that faculty should take on a social role that is about more than providing information from an unbiased or neutral stance. Referring to the natural scientist in the practice story, he said: "He has to help growers make a good decision and not be hoodwinked by a corporation that is going to want to sell something that might be very short sighted and profit driven." Rather than remaining neutral, this suggests that faculty should protect growers' interests against the interests of corporations.

This comment provoked a response from a full professor in a natural science discipline. Instead of working to protect growers' interests, she said, land-grant faculty should "work for the public interest." She argued that land-grant faculty members have "a unique opportunity and obligation to provide analysis on behalf of the public's point of view. That's our job, and for me, it ultimately traces back to democracy." The role of land-grant faculty in a democracy, she went on to say, is to serve "as an objective resource for accurate, thorough, considered analysis." Speaking of her own public engagement work as a plant breeder during the previous five years, she went on to say that "I felt I almost became an activist, but it was an activist on behalf of the public, of my perception or my interpretation of the public interest." In her view, then, land-grant faculty members must—and apparently can—simultaneously serve as "objective" resources and as advocates or activists on behalf of their personal interpretations of the public interest.

As members of the focus group continued to articulate and discuss their views and interpretations of the practice story, an associate professor in a natural science discipline offered some comments in which he positioned both himself and the faculty member in the practice story in a middle position between activist environmentalists, client groups (such as strawberry growers), and private corporations. Like the faculty member in the practice story, he said, "I have tried consistently to get myself in a middle position. I say what I think needs to be said, which is maybe not what either side wants me to say." According to him, what needs to be said comes not from his personal opinions or interests, but from his objective scientific knowledge and expertise.

The idea that the middle is the proper place for faculty to be as they engage in public work emerged not only in this focus group interview, but in other focus group interviews and many individual interviews. For example, in one of our focus group interviews that was devoted to a discussion of another practice story, an associate professor in a social science discipline said the following:

> I've gotten in a lot of trouble in ag groups for saying that it's the public's right to decide they want no pesticides used at all. They may be wrong, they may be right, I don't know. But it's their right. But what I insist on is that that decision be made on the information, on an informed decision-making process. They can still decide they don't want pesticides. To me, that's what we're all about.

Responding to these comments, an associate professor in a natural science discipline emphasized that by insisting on and participating in informed decision-making processes about difficult social problems, "we are functioning as agents for change. And I think that we can be an agent for change not by advocating a position, but by helping people to think about something differently."

Does it matter that most of the scholars we interviewed express conflicting and conflicted views about their political roles and stances? What is the meaning and significance of their desire to situate themselves in the middle? Is there such a place as the middle? These are some of the seriously difficult questions we need to be able to answer if we wish not only to understand but also to strengthen and defend the contemporary practice of public scholarship in land-grant colleges of agriculture.

Pessimism about the Future

The faculty members we interviewed are remarkably positive people. But when we asked them how well they think the kind of l ocalized engagement in public work they do is valued and supported, and where they see things heading in the future with respect to such work, many grew quite negative and pessimistic. Using their own experience or the experiences of those they know as evidence, many of them claimed that the work they do is not valued, supported, or pursued by most of their academic peers. In explaining why, they pointed to a variety of powerful internal and external barriers and disincentives, including a lack of rewards and money, a general lack of interest, a general unwillingness to expend the kind of energy and time it takes to be engaged in public work, the erosion of public funding, the decline (in terms of numbers and political power) of their core rural and agricultural constituencies, hiring patterns in their departments and colleges that reflect the research university norm of civic detachment, and the growing attraction of "big science" initiatives in molecular biology and genomics that tend to make working in local communities look trivial and outdated.

This is a bleak picture. If it is real rather than imagined, and if nothing is done to change it, the end result seems obvious. As a professor from a natural science discipline told me in response to a question I asked him about the future of the land-grant system's public engagement mission, "The whole thing is going to go away. People just aren't going to see the value."

Conclusion

The value for the general public of land-grant colleges and their affiliated experiment station and extension systems is too often viewed as being only economic in nature. To borrow again from William Sullivan, such a view reflects a wholly technical understanding of what the academic professionals who are employed by these colleges are about. This understanding is false. As I have demonstrated in this chapter, at least some of these professionals were and are about much more than this. They were and are about the pursuit of public work, ends, and ideals that are not only economic but also political, environmental, and cultural in nature.

In *The Sociological Imagination*, which was published in 1959, C. Wright Mills argued that the "educational and the political role of social science in a democracy is to help cultivate and sustain publics and individuals that are able to develop, to live with, and to act upon adequate definitions of personal and social realities." In my work of reconstructing a previously obscured tradition of public scholarship in land-grant colleges of agriculture, I am beginning to see why and how scholars in a variety of academic fields—including the natural as well as social sciences—have taken up this nontechnical educational and political role in their proactive, face-to-face engagement in public work. But I am also beginning to see what scholars are up against as they attempt to sustain this tradition into the future. Given the seemingly overwhelming power of the many disincentives and challenges they face, is there any real hope of success?[21]

With respect to this question, listen to Nick Jordan, a natural scientist who is a full professor in the Department of Agronomy and Plant Genetics at the University of Minnesota. In response to a question I asked him about what he and other public scholars are up against in Minnesota, he told me that "the most important challenge is that there is a rapid decline in public support for what we're doing. It's just very clear that we're not getting an adequate base of financial support for what we do here." He went on to speak of a "managed decline" in his college, the official name of which is the College of Food, Agricultural, and Natural Resource Sciences. In his view, this decline is a result of the "obsolescent story" his college

---

[21] C. W. Mills, *The Sociological Imagination* (New York: Oxford University Press, 1959), 192.

communicates to the public about agriculture, and the college's role in supporting it. "The obsolescent story," he says, "is that agriculture is about the production of commodities in an industrial mode, and that that's all it's about: that it's not about public health and it's not about environmental quality, and it's not about rural communities."

Jordan has been working hard with many of his colleagues to change this story. In reflecting on his experience, he offers those of us who believe in the value of public scholarship a glimmer of hope. "I'm hopeful," Jordan says:

> that we're developing what I think is an increasingly powerful and compelling case against current indus-trialized agriculture. This case is rapidly expanding beyond the traditional sustainability concerns of en-vironmental quality and rural community well-being to issues such as public health, children's health, and environmental quality that are compelling to a much larger group of people. I think that we are coming to connect our notions of how we should function differently as an agriculture college to a broader move-ment about how universities in general should function differently as engaged civic institutions.

In trying to understand the meaning and significance of what Jordan is saying here, I have come to realize that scholars in land-grant colleges who share Jordan's commitments must do more than simply practice a democratic tradition of public scholarship. Up against many oppositional forces and trends, they must also take up the task of reconstructing it. They must make a concerted effort to understand, strengthen, and defend its civic as well as academic purposes and value as one means of pursuing the land-grant mission.

In an important essay published in 1996, Eugene Rice spoke of the need to make a place for the "new American scholar." According to Rice, one of the defining characteristics of the new American scholar is deep engagement in rather than detachment from civic life. Ironically, in land-grant colleges the present challenge is to keep a place for a class of *old* American scholars, a class that has long embraced and enacted—however imperfectly—the pledge civic professionals' make to "deploy their technical expertise and judgment not only skillfully but for public-regarding ends and in a public-regarding way."[22]

---

[22] R. E. Rice, *Making a Place for the New American Scholar* (Washington, DC: American Association for Higher Education, 1996).

A Portrait of a University as a Young Citizen

Jeremy Cohen

> I will not serve that in which I no longer believe,
> whether it call itself my home, my fatherland, or my
> church; and I will try to express myself in some mode
> of life or art as freely as I can and as wholly as I can,
> using for my defense the only arms I allow myself to
> use, silence, exile, and cunning.
>
> *James Joyce*

"Once upon a time and a very good time it was there was a moo cow coming down the road," James Joyce began his largely autobiographical novel, *Portrait of the Artist as a Young Man*. The good times at Penn State, and very good times they have been, are legendary. A student will shout, *"We are!"* A louder *"Penn State!"* follows, not just the retort of a Saturday afternoon stadium chorus, but also the exuberant response of first-time visitors on campus tours who want to belong to the community, our community, even if only for the hour it takes to walk by the library, under the elms on the mall, across from the new glass and brick Information Science and Technology Building, always in earshot of the recorded carillon piped from the Old Main Tower, and ending at the T-shirt rack of the student store. Penn State, like Joyce's novel, rarely sits for an easy stereotype. The *Princeton Review* ranked Penn State the number two party school for 2006. That is part of the community's ethos. But there is more. *Washington Monthly*'s poll, ranking universities for their service to the nation, awarded Penn State the number 3 slot for the same 12 months.

Joyce blurred exploratory imagery of infancy through the complex intellectual coming of age of an Irish writer. An emerging Penn State faculty and student cohort are in their own ways also coming of age, struggling with questions about university mission and the academy's place in a society in which, some believe, the nation's democratic tenets are under siege. These faculty and students are asking *political* questions; questions, that is, about the nature of the ways in which we as a people live, the rules by which we organize ourselves in communities, the things we stand for, and our place as scholars in a university community and in communities with invisible borders that stretch beyond city or county or even nation-state. Their concern is with their agency as professional scholars, with their obligation to induct students into a community with obligations that reach beyond individual service, and with the public nature of the arts and sciences that underlie democratic

> *"We saw little likelihood of strong faculty involvement until the emphasis changed from service as a stand-alone, to scholarship and curriculum as a foundation for democratic practice."*
>
> ("Public Scholarship at Penn State: An interview with Jeremy Cohen," *HEX,* 2005.)

understanding and commitment. The patois of *public scholarship,* still a relatively new term that lacks a commonly accepted definition, nonetheless provides common ground—an invitation to others in its apparent recognition of shared concerns. Public scholarship, if it is not strictly speaking a philosophy or a set of tenets with an identifiable canon, is nonetheless an organizing principle that has helped some Penn State faculty to identify inherently political questions about their work and to build a collegial and supportive community to consider them.

Our university is a community in which, like Joyce's young artist, students and faculty are making decisions about whom or what to serve. Some, particularly undergraduates, are grappling with personal issues, such as religious faith, sexuality, artistic vision, race, ethics, and family and national loyalty. Purposeful and principled subscription to truly democratic modes of life are often submerged by the tides of what, to many young people, may seem like more pressing concerns. Motivations of professional advancement and disciplinary achievement germinating among graduate students are often well defined by the time they become faculty. Yet allegiances such as these, whether to personal growth, the university's athletic teams, or to discovery within formal domains of knowledge, are not inherent or predetermined traits. One way or another, individuals must choose the *home, fatherland,* or *church,* and the principles of democracy or the dictates of something else, they will serve. The essence of the paragraphs that follow is that the arts and sciences of knowledge are public, that they are a necessary keystone of American constitutional governance, and that professional educators have a constitutionally fashioned obligation to conserve and to nurture the interactions of knowledge and democracy through their teaching and their discoveries. Purposeful teaching and discovery that meets these goals will need to do more than frame democratic sovereignty as volunteerism.

The goal today is to capture some of these public scholarship questions and to suggest that a dedication to something larger than family, homeland, or church, is emerging at Penn State as educational practices increasingly referred to as *public scholarship*. Three deep upwelling currents are mixing in public scholarship's academic estuary: discovery, diffusion, and democratic engagement. All three are necessary to the sustainability of democratic capacity. Democratic capacity is composed of the knowledge and skills each generation requires to understand its democratic system and the civil obligations democratic organisms generate. Synthesis, creativity, and continual engagement also are necessary to sustain our scheme's political tenets of public sovereignty. Each element must be learned.

Public Scholarship and Democratic Capacity

Public scholarship is moving some of us away from satisfaction with service learning as an end in itself and from the land-grant mission in isolation as a *raison d'être* for our work. Penn State is not abandoning either service learning or land-grant outreach. Yet these practices alone are insufficient to build democratic capacity. Many faculty and students are finding service learning too often removed from the university's disciplinary scholarship foundations.

Land-grant practices do address scholarship diffusion and service but are far from central to a university's undergraduate instructional mission.

> *"Students are members of our academic communities—or at least, they should be."*
>
> ("Public Scholarship at Penn State: An interview with Jeremy Cohen," *HEX*, 2005.)

Democratic capacity requires civic engagement founded not on acts of charitable volunteerism, but on an instrumental obligation to bring discovery and diffusion—education—to bear on issues of public consequence. The acts of charity and selfless giving that often provide the motivation for service learning are marks of ethical commitment; they are to be applauded. They are—like the contributions of civic groups, congregations, and fraternal organizations—appropriate actions of students and other community members. Yet philanthropic and sweat-equity participation without deep knowledge and active engagement is not sufficient to fulfill the compact between higher education and democratic sovereignty. Charity begins with an individual ethic to help another. But democratic engagement is not an individual act of charity. It is a national (some would say international) *political obligation* to participate actively in democratic sovereignty. Education has a unique, value-added role to play.

Some of us—myself included—now believe that sustaining (some would say recapturing) our democracy is a core element and an obligation of our professional work. Explaining this requires focusing on complex relations between democracy and the Constitution. I have attempted to avoid unnecessary excursions into an arcane scholarship of constitutional theory and law. Nonetheless, focusing on public scholarship with no more than a passing reference to the complexity of democracy and its constitutional origins would be like discussing Joyce's *Ulysses* without reference to *The Dubliners* and *Portrait of the Artist*. One story goes that Joyce purposefully filled *Ulysses* with enough enigmas to keep "the critics busy for the next 300 years." Public scholarship rests on the notion that democratic capacity is derived not from a progression of historical enigmas, but from a purposeful recognition of the role of enlightenment in a sustainable democracy. The university's task is not to simplify democratic engagement by turning it into an act of community volunteerism or a democratic sound bite. The synthesis of discovery, diffusion, and democratic practice, like an atom's electrons, neutrons, and positrons, interact. Eliminating any element—discovery, diffusion, or democratic practice—alters the democratic chain reaction.

Public scholarship is neither an academic discipline, nor a one-dimensional pedagogy, nor another word for service. It is an idea. I said in a 2005 *HEX* interview that public scholarship ideas are derivative, links in a chain of science, humanities, and art that is hundreds of years old. I do not mean by that, however, that as a set of ideas or practices public scholarship is not also new, or at least a reimagination of education's role in building democratic capacity.

Some, perhaps contributing to this volume and many at Penn State, suggest that public scholarship is the revitalization of the land-grant mission. Neither history nor practice support that notion fully. The 1862 Morrill Act was pragmatic, instrumental, and fiscally far-sighted. Congress recognized the value generated by support for and maintenance of at least one college in each state:

> where the leading object shall be, without excluding other scientific and classical studies and including military tactics, to teach such branches of learning as are related to agriculture and the mechanic arts, in such manner as the legislatures of the States may respectively prescribe, in order to promote the liberal and practical education of the industrial classes on the several pursuits and professions in life.

It is fragmentary, however, to rest on the land-grant mission alone as the ethical, moral, legal, or normative rationale for Penn State's 21st-century public scholarship forays. The land-grant service ethos is only one tile within a finely detailed mosaic.

Beyond the Land-Grant: The Arts of Liberty

In fairness, it may be that the 1862 legislative intent Congress had in mind in promoting the "liberal" education of the industrial classes rested on the arts of liberty. James Madison spoke to the democratic value of liberal education a half century before President Lincoln signed the Morrill Act into law. He recognized the direct link between education and the ability of individuals to grapple with and understand the complex issues of self-governance. "Knowledge will forever govern ignorance; and a people who mean to be their own governors must arm themselves with the power which knowledge gives," Madison wrote. Madison was familiar too with the danger to individual liberties and democratic sovereignty inherent in any government unaccountable to the scrutiny of the public. Schools, Madison posited, provide the foundations of public accountability. "Learned institutions ought to be favorite objects with every free people," Madison said. "They throw that light over the public mind which is the best security against crafty and dangerous encroachments on the public liberty."

Within a university culture steeped in land-grant practice and service ideals, the impetus to change or to evolve from a service framework to a public scholarship paradigm can generate dissonance. Some suspect public scholarship is just another word for service learning or land-grant ethos. Others, primarily from student affairs, fear the *scholarship* emphasis. Will it displace their participation or reduce the commitment to the very service ideals they embrace?

The rationale for the semantic transformation from *service* and *outreach* to *public scholarship* is more than wordplay. We are in a period of reconceptualization of our academic work. Why is this necessary? Notions of the public good and of the university's role appropriately change over time. The second Land Grant Act, passed in 1890, continued the United States' apartheid treatment of blacks. "The establishment and maintenance of such colleges separately for white and colored students shall be held to be a compliance with the provisions of this act," Congress decided. Change was required to implement the act's true ideals.

Supreme Court Justice Thurgood Marshall delivered a speech in 1987, marking the bicentennial of the Constitution, that underscores the value of reinterpreting foundational tenets. "I do not believe that the meaning of the Constitution was forever 'fixed' at the Philadelphia Convention," Marshall said.

> Nor do I find the wisdom, foresight and sense of justice
> exhibited by the framers particularly profound. To the
> contrary, the government they devised was defective from
> the start, requiring several amendments, a civil war and
> momentous social transformation to attain the system of
> constitutional government, and its respect for the individ-
> ual freedoms and human rights we hold as fundamental
> today.

For us, a transformative question has been: are the pedagogical and
policy tenets of service learning and land-grant service sufficient to
provide a democratic capacity keystone?

Madison's emphasis on education as a means to build democratic
capacity, and Marshall's acknowledgement of the American democracy's transformational needs are useful academy reminders. The
North American revolutionaries were willing to challenge the status
quo and to risk what early modern English writers, including advocates of individual liberty, such as John Milton and John Locke, were
not: Thomas Jefferson, James Madison, Benjamin Franklin, and others
did not fear *We the People* and hence did not fear the public sovereignty
of democracy. They were willing to experiment. They recognized that
only a delicate balance of structural government balanced by the
capacity of the public to govern held out the pragmatic promise of
sustainable liberty.

Some of the roots of Penn State's take on public scholarship are
in the service ideals of the land-grant mission. The service-learning
movement has been an entry portal for others. But these gateways
are proving insufficient to sustain interests that go beyond direct social
service. The denial of tenure to junior faculty who have focused on
service and the common practice of rooting service learning in student
affairs rather than scholarly traditions have proven to be dysfunctional
conditions for scholars drawn to academic careers by the value—and
values of—scholarship itself. Where is the scholarship in service, they
ask? How can volunteerism replace the academic foundations of the
sciences, arts, and professions? Where is the purposeful democratic
learning in the land-grant? The lack of direct connection between
sustaining democratic ideals and the direct service of land-grant and

service-learning outreach are producing ferment. Faculty concern over the disconnect between their work and the personal constructs of professionalism that drew them to university careers have seeded thoughtful, sometimes difficult conversations about the scholar's professional mission in a democracy.

> *"The greatest threat to our liberties and to our national security may not be from any number of foreign individuals or isms that select terror and violence as their mode of conquest. Our own failure to adequately educate young people in the public duty of participation in the public affairs of the nation may be sufficient to render the Founders great experiment senile."*
>
> ("Public Scholarship at Penn State: An interview with Jeremy Cohen," *HEX*, 2005.)

Students, like many other Americans, also are increasingly pessimistic about the legitimacy of their government and about their own ability to affect their nation's governance. This too is sowing Penn State's public scholarship growth. Service draws many students, perhaps as a way to do *something* in what is otherwise seen a disengaged political environment. But other students are quite purposefully seeking something more than service opportunities from the university. They want to address the cause, as well as the results, of social and cultural impediments to human rights.

The development of a public scholarship community at Penn State is a direct response from faculty and students who believe that the modern research university's mission was not forever "fixed" by the land-grant acts, the German university model that produced great 20th-century research universities, or even the foresight of John Dewey, Clark Kerr, or Ernest Boyer. Neither service learning, nor fidelity to land-grant doctrine alone has been sufficient to address the university's obligation to generate democratic capacity.

If public scholarship, like service learning and land-grant outreach, is about the service of the academy to others, then precisely because it is located within the university it is also about the purposeful conservation of knowledge and the diffusion of knowledge *toward democratic ends*. The public scholarship sprouts fertilized by Penn State's rich land-grant service roots did not germinate in the 1862 Land Grant Act or the 1985 insight of Stanford president Don Kennedy, Brown president Howard Swearer, and Georgetown president Timothy Healy, that led to the invention of Campus Compact and the fertilization of the university service ethos. Penn State's public scholarship germinated in the framers' faith in the promise of sustainable liberty based on public sovereignty and on public sovereignty that is nourished by education as well as by experience. Service learning and land-grant policy nourish a university's best instincts. Democratic principle—a constitutional obligation in the United States—provides a foundation deep enough to move discovery, diffusion, and democratic practice from charitable good will to political obligation.

The comments that follow consider three formative elements of our public scholarship work: the distinction between learning about democracy and learning democratic sovereignty; the importance of viewing service and service learning as elements of a larger endeavor in which service is only one component; and the value of a grassroots infrastructure when institutional support is lacking. They are neither fully inclusive nor complete. I've borrowed, begged, and reported ideas without proper citation and credit from several colleagues, including Carol Colbeck, Rosa Eberly, Connie Flanagan, Patty Wharton Michael, David Riley, Emily Janke, Tina Brazil, and Lakshman Yapa, among others. My translations may not represent their views faithfully, let alone the views of my institution. These are my interpretations as an academic administrator, schooled in literature and creative writing during a time of political unrest at San Francisco State, and in First Amendment and behavioral communication scholarship at the University of Washington at the end of a cycle of constitutional rights expansion.

Democratic Studies or Democratic Capacity?

I'm not clear that there has ever been a golden age of democratic learning—that is, of *learning to be democratic*. We are finding at Penn State that the distinction is not trivial. With support from Kettering Foundation, we hosted two dozen colleagues in November 2004 for a National Public Scholarship Conversation. There was consensus around the claim that *democracy*, *social justice*, *community engagement*, and *diversity* should be part of the lexicon of public scholarship. Yet explicating terms such as these, and focusing on how to include them in the curriculum, was difficult.

A colleague, for example, wanted to follow up with a definition of *democracy* and wrote to me shortly after the two-day gathering. Professor Demos (yes, that's a made-up name to protect friendship and to focus on the point, not the individual) is a thoughtful and deservedly respected scholar. Perhaps unintentionally, Professor Demos' gadfly definition has helped us at Penn State to identify a public scholarship problem. Here is the relevant part of the note:

> As for a definition of democracy, I was just concerned in the beginning—but it did not prove especially crucial, I think, the way discussion moved—that people not take for granted that the best democracy is the one with the most people participating or the most people deliberating. My definition of democracy, like most, I think, blends the features of widespread participation with institutional mechanisms for keeping minorities from being trampled on. So my definition is something like —a system of political rule that rests on periodic elections in a system of competing political parties with guarantees of free speech and assembly in which government decisions are confined by adherence to the rule of law and a guarantee of individual rights against the state, usually acknowledged in a written constitution to which the government and the people are responsible.

> I love the energy and passion of the service learning/ public scholarship/civic engagement crowd. But—as I am sure is true with you or anyone at a research university—I am always engaged in an internal dialog in

meetings like this one between what I hear around the table and what I know the dominant university culture is asking: where's the beef in validated research results? That is, if I want to reward my faculty for doing "public scholarship," can you show me that these efforts result in useable new knowledge that passes muster with standard academic journals and publishers and academic review? If not, I have to judge this a well-meaning distraction from what the university should be up to.

I think there is or can be an answer to these questions—that is, I think, especially for the social sciences, but not only the social sciences, the answer is that sometimes public scholarship can absolutely improve scholarship at large. But this is more an article of faith than a demonstrated achievement, I think. Well, we'll see.

> *"We don't have a movement yet, but perhaps even better, we do have the makings of a sustainable scholarly community interested in what it means to prepare students and communities for enlightened democracy."*
>
> ("Public Scholarship at Penn State: An interview with Jeremy Cohen," *HEX,* 2005.)

At least for Professor Demos and for many colleagues in November 2004, *public scholarship, civic engagement,* and *service learning* were interchangeable terms. The priority for Professor Demos was neither university service (an important element of the land-grant and outreach models) nor helping the next generation to understand and to learn and adopt the practices necessary to sustain democratic sovereignty. The charge, Demos said, was to "locate the beef," the university's sustenance. Knowledge in this paradigm requires a test—in the era of No Child Left Behind and expanding federal and state intrusion to curriculum, "a tangible demonstration of outcomes." Professor Demos' suggestion—gauging the success of public scholarship as, *will the efforts "result in useable new knowledge that passes muster with standard academic journals and publishers and academic review?"*—rested on the assumption that research university missions were appropriately and forever fixed in the penumbra of (1) the German research model and Clark Kerr's master plan division of scholarship among insoluble and separate institutions of research, (2) K-12 teacher certification and terminal degrees, and (3) remedial and vocational campuses or junior colleges that ironically, yet appropriately, are today referred to as *community* colleges.

Democracy was a troubling concept. Our National Conversation did not sufficiently address it. Later, I raised the democracy question again, this time with the faculty program committee of Penn State's new public scholarship-based intercollege minor in Civic and Community Engagement. The minor's requirements included a newly developed lower division survey course called Fundamentals of Civic and Community Engagement, a capstone project, approved fieldwork in the community, and several electives individually tailored for each student with the assistance and approval of faculty mentors. Missing at the National Conversation, and when the program committee met, and in the minor's curriculum, was a sustained consideration of democracy itself—either what it is, or how to practice it. A democracy requirement should be made explicit, I thought. I wanted our faculty to state what we wanted students to understand about democracy and what bodies of knowledge and practice would best contribute to that learning. This is not a new or an original thought. CIRCLE, Campus Compact, and others sometimes distinguish between learning about democracy and learning its effective practice. Public scholarship requires both. But too often and intentionally or not on the part of institutions, there has been an unsupported assumption that volunteering in a community provides the knowledge and praxis necessary to sustain a complex constitutionally based democracy.

The program faculty settled on requiring at least one "public issues and democracy" course. The language reads:

> Public Issues and Democracy Courses investigate the
> roles academic disciplines play in their contribution to
> public debate and participation in civic issues and com-
> munity problem solving. Through the lens of specific
> academic disciplines and the examination of their civic

meaning and public purpose, these courses contribute to student understanding of the democratic process and the reciprocal relationship between academic and democratic practices. These courses may also promote civic and leadership skills through class deliberation and debate, as well as other classroom activities and assignments.

It was a compromise and, for me, a placeholder. Students can still complete our minor with little understanding of the Constitution and insufficient practice, making explicit connections between their academic work and their obligations as citizens. We are still working on this, however, and we are making progress.

More recently, an advising session with the student leader of a campus organization interested in increasing student engagement in issues of campus and pubic importance drew my attention to another democracy problem, one I think of as the *neutrality trap*. The student outlined plans to organize debates, to secure speakers on a variety of topics, and to develop student podcasts on myriad issues. Underlying her enthusiasm was a desire to ensure that each of the initiatives would be politically *neutral*—in her words, "to present facts, but not just opinions." At Penn State, and I think elsewhere, there has been a conscious effort to view neutral discussions as a positive attribute and *political* discussion as somehow outside of acceptable manners, or worse. Why? Political participation has become an invitation for derision. Our students have grown up in an environment in which political practice is reduced to vitriolic name calling. Opposition to the Iraq War is characterized as cut-and-run cowardice. *Liberal* has lost all connection to its semantic roots. The 2004 presidential election produced a new term, *swift-boating*, which refers to attacking the loyalty as well as the accuracy of political opponents. Both major parties, all three branches of government, and certainly the mass media have helped to bring this about. So has our failure in the schools to build democratic capacity that includes deep understanding of the positive political nature of democracy. Certainly the Constitution and democratic theory view practices relating to the government and to the public affairs of a democracy—politics—in a more favorable light.

No wonder students are having a difficult time distinguishing partisanship from the Constitution's implicit *political* compact that obligates citizens to be governors as well as the governed. Democratic governance is rife with political questions. Does the president have inherent authority to engage in what he refers to as a war against terror in whatever ways he sees fit? May the right of *habeas corpus* be eviscerated by administrative fiat or legislative action without violating the Constitution? The Constitution and two centuries of case law provide far more useful responses than the shriek of radio commentary or the oppressive censorship of neutrality. Learning to make sense of the political structure of a democratic system, however, takes sustained work—more than volunteerism alone. Our job as faculty is not to provide partisan responses, but it is to help students understand that questions involving war, taxes, health care, and civil rights are *political questions* and that the answers citizens *choose* have consequence. Choosing responses to political questions is part of learning to be a citizen in a democracy. *Learning* these democratic skills requires explicit knowledge and guided practice—no less so than learning math, language arts, or music. Somewhere, we have failed as educators to fully grasp the fact that nothing about democracy, not its theory and certainly not its practice, is hardwired into anyone.

The founders studied the work of the French *philosophes*, who studied not only the political sciences of the day but also the histories of the Romans and the Greeks and other failed and successful polities.

The separation of democratic learning from academic learning is further complicated today by high-profile attacks on the perceived politicization of the curriculum. When the Pennsylvania State Legislature launched formal hearings in 2005 into the alleged partisanship of faculty, Penn State conducted a study of the years 2000 to 2005. During those 5 years, 177,457 class sections were offered. Students had filed a total of 13 formal complaints about partisanship or other inappropriate faculty classroom activities. The dearth of specific instances of student complaints suggests strongly that there was neither partisan smoke nor political classroom fires fanned by either the right or the left. Yet in the spring of 2006, the faculty senate passed formal legislation to provide students with the *right* to challenge an instructor's alleged partisanship. Time will tell which is greater, the legislation's chilling effect on democratic learning, or its protection of rights. My office provided the procedures to implement "classroom freedom of expression and mediation." So far, I've had one student query. Isn't it unfair of biology faculty, the student wanted to know, to keep creationist beliefs out of a graduate biology seminar?

We are learning at Penn State that *democracy* is not a simple term to define, that it is a term worth explicating and that teaching democracy is not a simple idea to implement. None of those who spoke up at the public scholarship faculty meeting seemed comfortable with the challenge to formalize a democracy requirement. Some said they simply did not know how to teach democracy because democracy is not an element of their discipline. We are still trying, now more explicitly I think, to explicate what we mean by teaching students about democracy and then teaching them explicitly to take part in it. Our public scholarship activities have provided us with a forum, but not an answer to the question: how can a research university best teach democratic capacity?

From Service to Democratic Capacity

U. S. Supreme Court Justice Stephen Breyer, seeking a principled means to decide cases that generate conflicting views of the Constitution's intent, developed a doctrine he refers to as *active liberty*. He posits that democracy can be successful only when citizens participate. Breyer's judicial method examines the outcomes of a given constitutional interpretation, asking: how does this interpretation affect the ability of people to engage as citizens? He has applied the active liberty analysis to cases involving affirmative action, privacy, separation of church and state, and campaign finance.

Breyer does not stop with a theoretical axiom that the people have an obligation to participate in the democracy. His 2005 tract, *Active Liberty*, identifies a direct path between education and democracy. "The people, and their representatives," Breyer wrote, "must have the capacity to exercise their democratic responsibilities. They should possess the tools, such as information and education, necessary to participate and to govern effectively." Breyer's democratic mapmaking is a response to Justice Anton Scalia's 1997 manifesto, *A Matter of Interpretation: Federal Courts and the Law*, which posits allegiance to *originalism*—the doctrine that original intent, the exact words and beliefs of the framers—must control modern constitutional interpretation. These are incompatible doctrines.

In Scalia's democracy, the rule of law and the meaning of the Constitution are static, forever fixed. Breyer, like Thurgood Marshall, sees democracy as a living process. Citizens must not only build their democratic capacity to govern effectively, they must also use that capacity. Choosing between Scalia's originalism and Breyer's active liberty is a political decision. Deciding whether research universities will teach active liberty, or root themselves forever in 19th-century institutional models, is also a political question—one that faculties must play a primary role in deciding. Breyer's democratic capacity implicit in active liberty requires both democratic understanding and the ability to apply specific knowledge to issues of public import. Scalia's more passive view reduces the degrees of freedom and responsibility within the public's democratic role. Citizens need only to respect the rule of law, to volunteer in their communities, and to vote (a view expressed and favored by Attorney General Alberto Gonzales at the 2006 National Conference on Citizenship).

Historian Sean Wilentz prefaced his 2005 study of American democratic roots with a timely warning. "Democracy is never a gift bestowed by benevolent, farseeing rulers who seek to reinforce their own legitimacy," Wilentz said. "It must always be fought for by political coalitions that cut across distinctions of wealth, power, and interest. It succeeds and survives only when it is rooted in the lives and expectations of its citizens and is continually reinvigorated in each generation. Democratic successes are never irreversible." At Penn State, public scholarship has come to mean that as educators we cannot aid Breyer's democratic capacity building or the reinvigoration of democratic institutions, principles, and practices unless we move beyond simple notions of community service and volunteerism. Contributing to democratic survival is more complicated than being willing to serve.

Yet student service in the guise of volunteerism has taken on a life of its own in education. The talismanic view of service as independently capable of generating and sustaining democratic capacity is at best a fond hope. The habits of citizenship and comprehension of the political system to which we subscribe—like the curricula of language, fine arts, math, science, and the professions—can be learned and practiced in the academy. Higher education, at least in my view, is failing to root democracy into the lives and expectations of citizens. Young adults are learning to engage with their communities, if at all, through occasional individual acts of charitable volunteerism rather than through informed and sustained political practices of democracy.

Even with attention to public scholarship theory, however, teaching democracy is difficult. Students in Penn State's Foundations of Civic and Community Engagement course labored a good portion of a recent semester under the false impression that *public* was another word for *poor*. The students lumped together public welfare, public assistance, public housing, and public service and viewed service as charitable work to help the less fortunate—that is, the public. It required nuanced teaching far beyond the casual engagement of emotional journal reflection, supported by carefully drawn readings and explicit scholarship, to teach the class that in a democracy *We the People are the public*. Penn State public scholarship is trying to avoid the prospect of having students view democratic obligation as discrete, one-time service opportunities. You serve and you're done. We want instead to instill an understanding of citizenship that integrates students' use of their scholarship in all its disciplinary richness with a deep awareness of democratic obligations to address public (that is to say, common or shared) problems and to frame citizenship responsibilities as ongoing. Citizenship is something you do every day.

Infrastructure and Institutional Support

We have developed a Penn State community called the Public Scholarship Associates, which has grown from a literal handful of colleagues to scores of faculty, professional staff, graduate, and undergraduate students. I wrote to the Vice President for Under-graduate Education in 1999: "Public scholarship, sometimes referred to as service learning, involves the development of regular opportunities for students to apply their coursework and research to community issues of consequence." Since then, we've spent a fair amount of time thinking about why public scholarship is not service learning (although service learning pedagogies may be useful and effective components of a public scholarship curriculum). That is a narrative for another time.

Today I believe that public scholarship is a useful educational dialog in which the notion of the *public* refers to notions of public good, public ownership of discovery, and public obligations to democracy —all elements of democratic capacity and democratic sovereignty. Within this public scholarship explication, scholars and their institutions are members of the public. In the *International Encyclopedia of Youth Activism*, I wrote: "Public scholarship is the conduct of scholarly and creative work, including teaching, research, artistic performance, and service, in ways that contribute to informed engagement in the democratic process." The statement is purposefully broad—it explicates without forever defining—and it is not limited to public service. Rosa Eberly and I continued the explication in a visioning essay for the 20th anniversary of Campus Compact in 2006: "Rather than a prescriptive methodology, public scholarship is an educational philosophy in which the mission or desired university outcome is democratic capacity-building among students and contribution to democratic sovereignty by faculty, students, and staff. Public scholarship carries an explicit appreciation of education's special obligations and the value of fully integrating scholarship with democratic practice." We suggested that public scholarship universities should subscribe to three corollaries:

- Students must receive effective instruction in the theory and practice of democratic citizenship that includes appropriately focused scholarship as well as field practice.

- The public has a right to benefit not only from the infusion into the polity of citizens with democratic capacity nurtured by scholarship and instruction in democratic principle and practice, but also from the university's discovery and diffusion of new knowledge and practice applied to public needs and issues of local and national concern. This includes the scholarship and artistic contributions of faculty as well as students.

- The public's institutions of higher education must serve as conservators of the experiences, discoveries, understandings, and skills that are the essence of human enterprise and knowledge and that provide the enlightenment necessary for wise governance.

Today at Penn State, at least two doctoral students are undertaking dissertations about public scholarship. We offer a public scholarship minor on five of our campuses. We work under an umbrella called The Laboratory for Public Scholarship and Democracy, which includes a coordinator funded by the Office of Undergraduate Education. The laboratory sponsors a student club whose purpose is to increase awareness of, and participation in, issues of public importance. Several faculty public scholarship research projects are underway, and we are able to provide limited seed money for research, courses, professional travel, and fieldwork. Some of the details are available on our Web site (www.publicscholarship.psu.edu). These initiatives and others are useful artifacts of our consideration of what it means to develop democratic capacity. A recent volume deserves particular attention in the attempt here to describe what we are doing and why. *A Laboratory for Public Scholarship and Democracy*, edited by Eberly and me and published as a volume in the New Directions in Teaching and Learning series, presents research from six Penn State faculty and five graduate students and a concluding chapter from higher education reformer Judith Ramaley. The scholarship focuses on:

- the constitutional foundation of public scholarship

- the individual, organizational, and epistemological factors that shape faculty public scholarship engagement

- the ancient and contemporary connections between common space and public scholarship that cross disciplinary boundaries

- the developmental challenges and competencies of the early adult years and the scholarly basis for believing that public scholarship is an effective means of education for young adults in a democracy

- the direct links among professional school education, global citizenship, and field practice beyond the campus
- the explication of public scholarship constructs and objectives
- the epistemological limitations of traditional university practices and the potential inherent in the public scholarship practices some have adopted to replace them
- the developmental and educational links between public scholarship and the public decision making required by democracy

Each approach represents the fundamental work of scholarship. Each has been conducted, not as a good service add-on, but as a component of our work as professional scholars in a democracy. We are trying at Penn State to distinguish between the complexity of teaching and learning democracy and the simple and ethical decision to volunteer in a community. We've learned that the obligations the Constitution holds for professional educators are not passive. The idea of public scholarship has provided an instrument through which we have been able to begin to make the argument that teaching and learning democracy are obligations of membership in a democratic community and are at the heart of the civil fidelity entrusted to our schools and that the public diffusion of the discoveries and applications of our work as scholars, artists, and artisans is a foundation of politically responsible curriculum and pedagogy.

Confronted by the demands of his own conscience as well as the claims of others, Joyce's young artist came to understand his obligations as an artist. Public scholarship, we believe, is about nothing less than the obligations of educators and educational institutions to the duties of democratic sovereignty. In the face of research university practices that include economic pragmatism, a premium on personal advancement, and purposeful avoidance of political engagement, our democratic obligations are too often unmet. In a time of violent warfare in the name of democracy that has extended for a period longer now than the violence of World War II and that has usurped U.S. constitutional rights long held self-evident, it is incumbent upon scholars to revisit the duties of educational institutions and educators to the democratic practices that enable unfettered discovery.

Postscript

Randall Jarrell, a mid-20th century American author, wrote, "It is better to entertain an idea than to take it home to live with you for the rest of your life." I fear that phrases like *public scholarship*, *service learning*, and others are cases in point. They have institutionalized themselves in our academic homes and not without cost. Public scholarship may provide a useful heuristic—but the real issue is not about convenient phrases to dissect. *We the People* as a political body and the People's loss—our forfeiture—of democratic sovereignty are the issues at stake. Education, through teaching, discovery, the conservation of the arts and sciences, and through the diffusion of knowledge, carries obligations to the next generation largely unmet by our institutions of higher education. Universities can provide public commons in which the knowledge domains, the practices, and the skills of democratic sovereignty are taught and disseminated as a coherent whole. To do so will require a reimagining of our roles in which learning democratic capacity will be as important as the domains of knowledge that support it. Discovery, the conservation of the arts and sciences, the diffusion of knowledge, and their placement in a meaningful and socially responsible context are the substance of democratic capacity. The affirmative constitutional obligation of professional educators is to ensure that that capacity does not run dry.

CHAPTER FIVE

Public Making: The Perspective and a Story

The Makings of a Public and the Role of the Academy

The New England Center for Civic Life—A Decade of Making a Difference

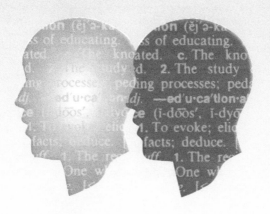

The Makings of a Public and the Role of the Academy

Noëlle McAfee

For more than a decade, those embarking on public scholarship and those rethinking the civic mission of the university have been asking, what kind of relationship should there be between the academy and the public? This is much bigger than the old town/gown problem. It is more than a matter of building good public relations. And the closer one looks at it the more complex this "relationship" becomes. We are not asking about the relationship between one thing and another thing, for neither the academy nor the public is a thing. The academy is not only spread out all over the world, not only a loose unfederated array of institutional and scholarly inquiries with a mission to teach, to learn, and to serve; it is a frame of mind, a way of relating to the world as it is, and it is often situated in something like a hierarchical relationship to all it studies and to whom it teaches.

But what is even more intriguing and baffling is this non-thing we call "the public": most always with the definite article, *the* public. To use the term *publics*, as some with multicultural sensibilities sometimes do, is to twist the word beyond recognition, for the word *public* seems designed to connote a collectivity, really an ubercollectivity of members of a political community (at whatever scale); and if there is more than one collectivity, then any one of them isn't a collectivity or a public at all. Instead of a public, we might call it a faction.

I say the public, whatever it is, is not a thing. By that I mean that it is not waiting in the wings. It is ephemeral. It comes together one day, it seems, and disperses the next. A public is always in relation to something else, whether a problem that can, upon recognition, band people together, or a cultural production, or a speech. Yet with speeches and cultural productions, "a public" seems to mean anyone paying attention, and it calls for little more than paying attention. That's what we call an audience, not a public.

The public scholarship movement is part of a larger civic renewal movement. So the question is what kind of civic relationship there might be between the academy and the public. And so we need to try to understand what this public is in a civic dimension rather than a spectator sense. But civically speaking, there is a widespread concern that, perhaps, as Walter Lippmann claimed, the public is a phantom. We invoke the phantom public to make ourselves feel that we have a real democracy. But look around, he noted, people seem to be unable to fathom the complexities of the problems that beset them, much less are they able to engineer solutions. They barely know what is going on. They are like the theatergoer who shows up in the middle of the second act and leaves before the curtain closes, having stayed just long enough to figure out who the villains and the heroes are.

Well, maybe you are right, John Dewey replied. The public is inchoate, but this is largely because people have not found a way to fathom the problems that beset them—and each other. "At present, many consequences are felt rather than perceived," Dewey wrote; "they are suffered, but they cannot be said to be known, for they are not, by those who experience them, referred to their origins.... Hence the publics are amorphous and unarticulated."[1] To become a public, people need something that brings them together as a public. "An inchoate public is capable of organization only when indirect consequences are perceived, and when it is possible to project agencies which order their occurrence."[2] When people seem unable to cohere as a public, to grasp problems or identify solutions, the remedy is not to take away their authority. The remedy, Dewey argued, is to find ways to help the public find itself.

Identifying problems and beginning to see how these problems affect them and their fellows starts to help a public find itself. Dewey noted two other processes that need to happen: the public needs to be able to produce a knowledge of what could be done to address these problems, knowledge that might take the form of public opinion,

---

[1] John Dewey, *The Public and Its Problems* (Swallow Press, 1954), 131.
[2] Ibid.

public judgment, or public will, knowledge that ideally could help shape public policy; and second, members of the public need to be able to communicate together to help create this public knowledge.

> Systematic and continuous inquiry into all the conditions which affect association and their dissemination in print is a precondition of the creation of a true public. But it and its results are but tools after all. Their final actuality is accomplished in face-to-face relationships by means of direct give and take. Logic in its fulfillment recurs to the primitive sense of the word: dialogue.[3]

The public can find itself, or to put it more aptly, *make* itself by coming together to talk about the pressing problems of the day, to identify the sources of problems, to see how these problems differentially affect others, to try to decide together what should be done. Out of these processes, processes that all amount to what we call public deliberation, might emanate informed public opinion about what should be done. This information has a special status. Dewey put it this way, "The man who wears the shoe knows best that it pinches and where it pinches, even if the expert shoemaker is the best judge of how the trouble is to be remedied."[4] Public problems are best fathomed by the public itself. It may enlist experts or governments to fix the problems, but it alone is the best judge of what needs to be addressed and whether the remedy is successful.[5]

Dewey's clarification still left us with many problems. For one, how in fact the public can make itself, what help it needs, who can help, and how. For another, how it creates its intelligence, opinion, or judgment. And finally, how the public's understanding of what should be done can have any impact on those in the business of governing. While Dewey might have had a nice rejoinder to Lippmann, history took its cue from Lippmann, not Dewey, and the political system generally proceeds as if citizens are merely clients, taxpayers, and occasional voters, not potential publics with any

---

[3] Ibid., 218.

[4] Ibid., 207.

[5] Noëlle McAfee, "Public Knowledge, " *Philosophy and Social Criticism*, 30:2 (2004): 139-157.

valuable knowledge or authority to shape public policy. In the remainder of this chapter I take up these problems with an eye to how higher education may be an ally.

> *"The public is not a phantom. It is a pheno-menon that can be—and is, more often than we realize—generated by a set of public ideas, occasions for public deliberation, and institutions through which the public can find itself."*
>
> ("Getting the Public's Intelligence," *HEX*, 2004.)

A public makes itself performatively. It is in the process of doing public work that people become public. Recently I heard a talk in which the author made such a claim about the body itself.[6] If we notice what happens when a part of the body is immobilized, say, when a broken arm is put into a cast, we notice that over time, even as the bone heals, the muscles atrophy. And even after the bone mends, its strength is only recovered when it is repeatedly tested. Physical therapy involves putting the body to work precisely when and where it is not yet up for that work. The bone is not healed until it is able to withstand stress, and it only can come to withstand stress by doing this work when it's not ready. It becomes a body by "bodying." The body is an effect of a body working.

Likewise for the public. Writing in the 2004 issue of the *Higher Education Exchange*, David Mathews proposes:

> A sovereign or democratic public comes into being only when people begin to do the work of citizens, which Harry Boyte of the University of Minnesota calls "public work." This way of conceptualizing the public sees it as a dynamic force rather than a static body of people.... In other words, the public doesn't just do the work—doing the work creates the public.[7]

---

[6] David Morris, "The Body as the Institution of Temporality and as the Temporality of Institution," Merleu Ponty Circle, Washington, D.C., October 27, 2006.

[7] David Mathews, "Afterword: 'What Public?'" *Higher Education Exchange* (2004): 87-88.

The problem with a performative answer to the question of how a public makes itself is, ultimately, a chicken-egg problem, where to begin. If public making occurs through a public working, how did this public find itself in the midst of this work? If public making, as Mathews writes, "isn't separate from collective knowing, deciding (deliberating), and acting"; if "it *is* those activities," how does it find itself there?

I think it goes like this: individuals become a public when they come together with their individual opinions, preferences, and complaints and begin to talk together. Or whenever they are thrown together and start to put together how and why they were thrown together. A few years ago I heard an Argentinean woman describing a moment, standing in line outside the bank doors, when once again the political system was in crisis and the financial markets in turmoil. She was standing in line with hundreds of other people similarly worried about their savings, and then she and others looked around and at each other and began to identify themselves as a public *created* in this moment of recognition, of this connecting of the political crisis, the financial crisis, and their collective welfare.

If individuals are treated only as individual complainants, or even as an individual citizen to be surveyed, addressed, assured, a public cannot come into being. If politics proceeds by surveying individual preferences or adding up individual votes, nothing like public work can take place. The major problem of our day is that Lippmann and later Joseph Schumpeter convinced political thinkers and leaders that democracy can take place so long as individual views are aggregated and public policy is consistent with this aggregation. But this view of democracy is more about satisfying individuals, like a well-functioning market (in fact, it entirely takes its cue from market logic), and not at all about rule by the people, that is, if we are to think of "the people" as some kind of collective public.

There are two problems here: One is that the aggregated sum of individual views is inferior to the public understanding that comes about when people compare notes together. An aggregated sum adds up partial perceptions and blind spots; but public understanding results when people begin to fill in and interconnect partial views.

When people deliberate together about issues, an integrative process takes place. Together they unfold a problem through the back-and-forth of conversation, offering perspectives, anecdotes, and concerns. As this process goes on for a while, participants create an understanding of the topography of a political issue and they begin to see how various options would or would not be able to navigate that terrain. No aggregation of preferences on an issue could ever approximate what deliberation produces.[8]

The other problem is that aggregating individual views does not do any of the work of deciding what should be done. The task of politics is ultimately to decide what to do, work that still has to occur after an aggregation; but in this model the work is done by officials, not the public.[9] Unlike democracy, here officials take the aggregation of individual views *under advisement* as *they* do the work of deciding what to do. In a democracy, it is the considered opinion or judgment of the people, the *demos*, the *demes* that charts the course.

Despite the hold that Lippmann and Schumpeter's desiccated notions of democracy have on us, there is something still about public opinion that has an even stronger hold. Politicians continually refer and defer to it, even well between election cycles. There seems to be some kind of democratic ideal that gives public opinion gravitas even as the usual ways of gathering public opinion leave much to be desired. Asking a mass of individuals for their views, views that have never been tempered through public deliberation, and then tabulating the results delivers a table of preferences, not a *public* opinion.

Putting this more poetically, Jacques Derrida writes, "public opinion is *de jure* neither the *general will* nor the *nation*, neither *ideology* nor the sum total of *private* opinions analyzed through sociological techniques or modern poll-taking institutions."[10] No public comes

---

[8] See David Brown's interview with me in the 2004 issue of the *Higher Education Exchange*.

[9] Noëlle McAfee, "Three Models of Democratic Deliberation," *Journal of Speculative Philosophy*, 18:1 (2004).

[10] Jacques Derrida, "Call It a Day for Democracy," in *The Other Heading*, 87 (Bloomington, IN: Indiana University Press, 1992). Also *Kettering Review* (Fall 2003).

into being through aggregation. If public opinion is to be more than "the silhouette of a phantom," to borrow Derrida's wonderful phrase, it must be something other than the aggregation of private opinions. Instead of asking individuals what they think, people need to come together to decide what to do, to render a judgment on matters affecting the polity:

> Opinion, as its name indicates, is called upon to pronounce itself by means of a judgment. This judgment is not some knowledge, but an engaged evaluation, a voluntary act. It always takes the form of a "judgment" (yes or no) that must exercise power of control and orientation over this parliamentary democracy.[11]

The ideal of public opinion is that it might guide public policy, that the people might be ultimate arbiters of what the polity should do, where its policies should go. The democratic hope is that public opinion might be both authoritative and more able to grasp what is at stake than elected officials might.

> As the place of a potential electorate, public opinion is an assembly of citizens called upon to decide, by means of a judgment, issues that are within the competence of legal representation, but also issues that escape them, at least provisionally, in a zone that is being extended and differentiated today in an accelerated way, thereby posing serious questions about the present functioning, if not the very principles, of liberal democracy.[12]

The problem today is that the representative system of liberal democracy produces a gap between the public and its representatives, and any opinion that a public manages to form must find a way to be represented, and heard, by these representatives; representatives who no longer have much interest in heeding or taking seriously what the public might deem important.

But I am getting ahead of myself.

The mystery, if there is a mystery, of how a public performatively creates itself is not in its finding itself doing the work. It is no mystery

---

[11]Derrida, "Call It a Day for Democracy," 90-91.

[12] Ibid., 91-92.

that people might occasionally come together to talk—though we could certainly use more opportunities and occasions. The mystery may be in the work itself. What is this work? What is this public doing? Derrida says it is judgment, not a knowledge. It is a deciding what should be, not an ascertaining of what is true or false.

> *"When people deliber-*
> *ate face-to-face, they are*
> *called to respond to so*
> *much more than 'what' is*
> *said; they also respond to*
> *the humanity of others in*
> *the room."*
>
> ("Getting the Public's Intel-
> ligence," *HEX,* 2004.)

Compare Derrida's view to that of one of the leading theorists of deliberative democracy, Jürgen Habermas, as he criticizes the communitarian movement. Notice how Habermas disparages deliberation aimed at public self-understanding and public making in favor of deliberations aimed at reaching understanding about what is universally right for all (the moral equivalent of "true or false," not the ethical judgment Derrida calls for). "According to the communitarian view, there is a necessary connection between the deliberative concept of democracy and the reference to a concrete, substantively integrated ethical community,"[13] writes Habermas, borrowing Hegel's language about an ethical community. Where an ethical community (*sittlichkeit*) is concerned with what is good for itself, a moral order (*moralität*) is concerned with what is universally good for all. Political philosophers term these concerns ethics versus morality (rather confusing since usually these terms are indistinguishable), as well as "the good" (what is good for us) versus "the right" (what is just or right for all). Habermas favors focusing on universal morality rather than particular notions of the good. His worry about communitarianism's use of deliberation is that it is focused on particular attachments, not universal justice. In Habermas' view, the communitarian focuses on the ethical community in its deliberations because:

---

[13]Jürgen Habermas, "the Normative Models of Democracy," in Democracy and Differnce, ed. seyla Benhabib (Princeton, NJ: Princeton University Press, 1996), 24.

> Otherwise one could not explain … how the citizens'
> orientation to the common good would be at all
> possible.… The individual can get a clear sense of
> commonalities and differences, and hence a sense of
> who she is and who she would like to be, only in the pub-
> lic exchange with others who owe their identities to the
> same traditions and similar formation processes.[14]

The communitarian's focus on "the clarification of collective
self-understanding," says Habermas, "does not sit well with
the function of the legislative processes they issue in."[15] In-
sofar as collective deliberations are about regulating our lives
together, that is, about law, they should focus on universal
principles of justice, Habermas argues.

> To be sure, discourses aimed at achieving self-
> understanding—discourses in which the participants
> want to get a clear understanding of themselves as mem-
> bers of a specific nation, as members of a locale or a state,
> as inhabitants of a region, and so on; in which they want
> to determine which traditions they will continue; in
> which they strive to determine how they will treat one
> another, and how they will treat minorities and marginal
> groups; in short, discourses in which they want to get
> clear about the kind of society they want to live in—
> such discourses are also an important part of politics.
> *But these questions are subordinate to moral questions* … [em-
> phasis added], questions of justice. The question having
> *priority* in legislative politics concerns how a matter can
> be regulated in the equal interest of all.[16]

In Habermas' ideal politics, questions of universal moral validity,
that is, justice, take precedence over questions of solidarity. Habermas
subordinates deliberation aimed at choosing what kind of community we would like to be to the supposed priority of deliberation
aimed at questions of justice. The distinction itself is fine, at least
for analytical purposes; but the notion that these can be engaged
independently of one another is wrong. Whenever people deliberate
about what kind of community they want to be, they are addressing

---

[14] Ibid.

[15] Ibid.

[16] Ibid., 24-25.

matters of justice. And whenever questions of justice are on the table, they are approached in the context of a *particular* community's concerns. A political community addressing an issue of immigration is simultaneously struggling to integrate its desire to stand for openness and freedom with the exigencies, whether real or felt, of limited resources. Communities that are deliberating about how to "treat minorities and marginal groups" are very much involved in questions of justice while at the same time struggling with forging their own self-understanding. What I or we stand for is very much a part of who I or we are. Questions of justice weigh on the community's struggle to define itself. In such cases, deliberations turn on how to forge a particular community that upholds values that all might be proud of upholding. Our own self-understanding is tempered by what we think others will think of us, and most of us want to be seen as member of a moral order. So deliberation aimed at forging collective purposes is always already wrapped up with questions of more universal morality.

Moreover, it is these very deliberations aimed at deciding what kind of community we want to be that turn a people into a public, a public that might also take up questions of justice. Unless a public makes itself in the public work of deciding what it ought to do on matters of common concern, there will be no public to adjudicate questions of justice.

Michael Sandel made a similar point in his rejoinder to John Rawls's *Theory of Justice*. Like Habermas, and also following Kant, Rawls prioritizes the right over the good, universal principles of justice over particular concerns of a given community. Sandel argues that questions of justice are posed somewhere, in some particular context, among some particular people. The public work that makes a people a public is as vital as the public work of deciding matters of justice, and probably prior to it as well.

I asked earlier about this work that makes people a public; what kind of work is it? Derrida in his writing on public judgment said it was a judgment, a yes or no, not a knowledge. Likewise, Aristotle long ago noted that choice and deliberation in politics are about matters that have no certain answer. We deliberate about what we should do. We deliberate well when we have a sense of what good ends are, and these too can only be arrived at through practical deliberation, not scientific knowledge.

> "The ancient view of conversation holds that reasoning itself is a social event. We reason with others through our conversing, not merely in the presence of others."
>
> ("Getting the Public's Intelligence," *HEX*, 2004.)

Yet the form that Habermas' political questions take is more akin to questions of knowledge than questions of purpose. In fact he is quite explicit about this. Normative questions can be answered formally and cognitively, and their answers are either universally valid or not. These answers are found through the back-and-forth of conversation when all who are potentially affected have an opportunity to weigh in on whether the proposed policy would be best for all. Ultimately, in this round-robin conversation, the force of the better argument will prevail.

Note how different this is from the "engaged evaluation" that Derrida says is called for in forming public opinion.[17] Recall: "this judgment is not some knowledge, but an engaged evaluation, a voluntary act. It always takes the form of a 'judgment' (yes or no)." Habermas also sees the end result of deliberation as forming a kind of public opinion—public will—that, normatively, should exercise control of sorts over parliamentary politics. But where Derrida's public judgment is formed through engagement, decision, a yes or no, Habermas' is formed through a cognitive appraisal of which policy is right, an appraisal that will lead to unanimity on which policy meets the test of universalizibility. The less tainted by parochial concerns, by matters of solidarity and self-understanding, the better.

Does a public form itself in a Habermasian deliberation? In the back-and-forth of argumentation, there is little room for the sharing

---

[17] Op cit., 90.

of perspectives that can be integrated into a better understanding of the whole. In fact, coming to deliberation with partial perspectives is detrimental, Habermas thinks, to deliberation aimed at reaching understanding and agreement. Habermas' model of the deliberative forum is more like a logic class; where the Derridean, and I'd add Deweyan, one is more like a literature class. English professor Peggy Prenshaw described her own experiment in bringing deliberation to literary studies in an article she wrote for the 1998 issue of the *Higher Education Exchange*. Through a project on the humanities and public deliberation, she thought through the relationship between understanding literature and deliberating on public policy:

> The comparison I am pursuing here is that of the empirical undecidability of the questions raised by the text and a similar undecidability of public policy questions raised in citizens' forums. Resolution is reached by persuasion, by enlisting empathetic agreement, by noting facts, recalling historical precedents, reporting relevant personal experience, raising questions about the language and actions manifest in the text. An interpretation of a literary text, like a group's response to discussion of a public issue, is an act of judgment, an act that is language-bound, culture-bound. It is contingent on the disposition of a group of individuals in a given place at a given moment.[18]

In both forums and literature classes, the conversation can ramble, it will tarry on particular cases and focus on odd details. But most important in both kinds of conversation is a kind of "work of ascertaining the *meaning* of the data and texts."[19]

Prenshaw's observation is vital to understanding the gulf between deliberations aimed at universal answers and deliberations that can give rise to a public and public judgment. The former try to strip themselves of particularity; the latter try to unearth the richness of particularity. This richness has two sides: there are the

---

[18] Peggy W. Prenshaw, "Humanities Study and Public Deliberation," *Higher Education Exchange* (1998): 67.

[19] Ibid.

manifold aspects of a problem itself as well as its consequences for all concerned; and there is the meaning it has for all of us in connection with our own ever-evolving values, concerns, and purposes. When we look for the meaning of an event or a problem, it is not just what *it* means but what it means *for us*. Earlier I described how public deliberation helps elucidate the topography of a problem. In fact, in deliberations a seemingly inordinate amount of time is spent trying to understanding the problem itself (whether it's crime, immigration, the U.S. role in the world, or anything else). This may be the case because understanding the problem, and its meaning for us, is not just a matter of excavation and discovery but also of creation and interpretation. In articulating what a problem means for us, we also begin to articulate (both retrospectively and prospectively) the meaning of "us": who we are, what we want to stand for, with whom we are in relation.

This hermeneutic, interpretive aspect of public deliberation may explain how this work helps to create a public. Like the broken limb that is healed in returning to its function, in bearing weight, the public is formed by connecting disparate people through a process of forging meanings that connect people to each other and delineate possible courses of action. Any course of action will continue the process of public formation, and so with trepidation and anything but universal certitude we make our choices.

So what might be a civic relationship between the academy and the public? I'd say that it might be for the academy to be an ally in creating opportunities and ideas that support public making. The new chapter in this relationship, as documented in the pages of the *Higher Education Exchange*, has focused on creating new meanings of public scholarship and resurrecting old civic missions of the university as well as new opportunities to organize publics. But I caution against this "organizing" model. The occasions are good and welcome. But only a public can make itself into a public. If someone else leads the effort, then the very idea of a public as a creator of will and judgment is undermined. But the academy can be an ally, in no small part by continuing its own research and teaching with a newfound respect for public work.

It is in and through the academy that knowledge gets its stamp of approval; and in our continuing hangover from positivism, "opinion" and even "judgment" are deemed the lesser cousins of knowledge and certitude. The academy, as an ally to the public, can take a lead in changing this landscape. The humanities, as Prenshaw notes, are natural allies. But also are the natural sciences, as Scott Peters has found, in respecting the wisdom that a public can bring to even the most technological issues.

> *"Ultimately isn't that why people come together —not because they see themselves as budding epistemologists trying to discover 'the truth' but rather as political beings trying to discover a better way of living with others?"*
>
> ("Getting the Public's Intelligence," *HEX*, 2004.)

Whatever the means, the model of "allies" I think is worth exploring. It avoids the old hierarchical relationship between expert and public. It suggests that each party has its own work to do. It allows for each to do its own work fully without pretending to be doing the work of the other party. The academy can be an ally to the public, during both the times when it is little more than a phantom and during the times when it has something to say. During these latter times, when public judgment and will are being articulated but no one is listening, academic allies can serve as translators and representatives of public judgment, ever mindful to how any attempt at representation carries much responsibility to be faithful to the original, to try to let it speak, even if this is never quite fully possible.

During the former times, when the public is little more than a phantom, the job of the public scholar is much like the job of the public journalist who, as the late Cole Campbell noted, does not merely inform the public but serves as an asset in helping the public form itself. "Rather than settle for transmitting expert or elite knowledge," Campbell writes, the aim of the public journalist will be:

> to generate *public knowledge*, produced by a public's
> use of reason and experience. "Knowledge," in this
> usage, is not a commodity that can be stored up and
> transmitted as needed; rather, this is a kind of knowl-
> edge constantly being generated by—and in turn
> generating —new insights among citizens, experts
> and elites working with each other as a community.[20]

The public scholar can be an ally and a "shared asset," as Campbell
puts it, to a public working on pulling together an understanding of
itself, of its challenges, alternatives, and possible directions. Such
public work may pull the academic away from his or her usual ob-
ject of attention—whether medieval art or astrophysics—or it
might involve reorienting one's work in a public direction. What a
public scholar can share is not just what he or she knows but how
he or she comes to know and continues to generate and translate
meaningful work.

---

[20] Cole C. Campbell, "Journalism and Public Knowledge," *Kettering Review* (Winter 2007).

The New England Center for Civic Life—A Decade of Making a Difference

Douglas F. Challenger

Breaking the Logjam between the Public and the Public Schools

The headline in our local newspaper the *Monadnock Ledger* read: "J-R: Yes to bond." "J-R" stands for the names of the two neighboring towns (Jaffrey and Rindge) to Franklin Pierce University where I teach and have helped foster public deliberation on and off campus for the better part of the last 10 years. The headline was for an article reporting the results of the recent March 2006 elections during which the two towns, partners in a cooperative regional school district, passed the first major bond in many years for the purpose of school renovations. The school superintendent, James O'Neill, said, "We've made a tremendous move forward."

The back-story to this headline is interesting because it illustrates the idea and approach to democratic social change that the New England Center for Civic Life (NECCL) at Franklin Pierce University has been teaching and practicing since its inception in 1998. For many years, the local school district has felt a need to improve the Jaffrey-Rindge Middle School and Conant High School housed on the same small campus in the heart of the village of Jaffrey. Many proposals have been put forward in the last decade, but the idea school officials and many citizens championed was to build a new high school on land purchased by the school district in 1989, located on a stretch of rural road between the two towns.

Various versions of this plan were put before the local voters only to be rejected year in and year out from 1999 to 2004. During this time, citizens in both towns grew more and more divided each year the warrant articles were rejected at the polls. Three years ago in 2004, the election was particularly divisive as advocates for and against the new high school organized and aggressively worked to promote their positions. During the year leading up to the election, advocates formed into activist organizations, each mounting an impressive, multifaceted public relations effort to persuade citizens in the towns to take their side. As election time drew nigh, a "sign war" along the roadsides of the region made the division visible to all, especially when it was clear that each side had their signs vandalized and torn down by their opponents.

The advocates for the new school felt the current buildings were not large enough or modern enough to meet the educational needs of the region's growing school-age population. They thought those who opposed the bond issue for a new high school (and a renovated middle school at the site of the existing two schools) were basically voting against improved education out of self-interest in keeping their property taxes from getting higher. The school board and the advocates for a new school worked harder than ever in 2003-2004 and hoped for a positive electoral result that spring. But they were defeated by an even greater margin than the year before.

It was then that David Drouin, a citizen on the "pro new school" side of the dispute made a phone call to Jason Czekalski, a citizen from the group against that particular solution. They had been trading barbs in letters to the editor of the local newspaper during the run up to the election. "We've got to talk," Drouin said. Czekalski agreed. Two weeks later at the next school board meeting, they offered their idea to convene a citizens committee made up of members of both sides of the issue and asked the school board for their support. At that meeting, a community leader named Patricia Barry, who had worked with me and my students on a previous school/community Study Circles project in 1999, stood up and suggested that the group seek the help of the New England Center for Civic Life (NECCL).

School superintendent O'Neill had been involved with that Study Circles project, too. He had later attended a National Issues Forums (NIF) forum at Franklin Pierce University on "Public Schools: Are They Making the Grade?" and had come away from the event impressed at how the process enabled people to listen to each other's different views and to find some common ground through their deliberations. Exacerbated by the limitations of other advocacy-based civic engagement efforts, he wondered whether some version of that deliberative dialogue process might help the factions within the Jaffrey-Rindge School District build a bridge that would lead to greater community support of the district's public schools.

When NECCL got the call for help in April 2004, director Joni Doherty proposed the use of the Sustained Dialogue process developed by Kettering Foundation Director of International Affairs Harold Saunders. It was a process we had used successfully for years at Franklin Pierce University with students and faculty to talk about tensions related to racial/ethnic and other kinds of social diversity within the campus community. The citizens' committee liked the process she proposed and invited Doherty to help them get started.

They began meeting once a week from May through August.

> *"Rather than aiming at knowledge representative of a collection of individuals, the practices of deliberative democracy attempt to create legitimacy through the establishment of a public voice that reflects the common ground among them."*
>
> ("Living in the Lap of an Immense Intelligence: Lessons on Public Scholarship from the Field," *HEX*, 2002.)

Doherty was the facilitator at first, but soon turned that role over to coleaders representing each of the two groups. She helped them agree on a name—Citizens Seeking Common Ground—offered meeting space at Franklin Pierce University for the group to use and coached them in how the dialogue process works. The weekly dialogue helped the members begin to better understand the perspectives of those with whom they disagreed. As the weeks turned into months, members from both sides deepened their understanding of each other and began to see the issue in more complex terms and to view each other as real people, each with many legitimate concerns and good ideas. Eventually, they saw that they shared many of the same values and hopes for their communities. They were propelled forward by a belief that common ground could be forged without compromising their ideals.

The "pro-school" group saw that the "anti-school" group was not against improving education so much as they just wanted to make sure the school board and officials were being financially responsible to the town's middle- and lower-income residents with their idealistic plans. They also did not want the existing school to move out of their community —it was a hub of local life and an important component of efforts to maintain a vibrant community and revitalize their town center. They were also concerned about all the intangible social costs to students and to the town of Jaffrey of moving the school out of the village center to the "suburbs" and changing it from a community-based school to what seemed to them a more anonymous, campus-style one.

> *"The kind of politics that makes citizen deliberation central to democracy trusts the public's experience and intelligence as a vital resource, and seeks to nurture that intelligence and give it opportunity for development and expression."*
>
> ("The College as Citizen: One College Evolves through the Work of Public Deliberation," *HEX*, 2000.)

The pro-school citizens had wanted the new school to be located at a new site on the land between the two towns and had not understood how much of the opposition to the idea of building a new school was related to concerns about its proposed location. On the other hand, those who were voting year after year against the proposal for a new school began to see how serious the needs were for more space and better facilities. And they realized how important it was to be part of a solution, instead of standing in the way of change. They realized that what appeared like stubborn belligerence on the part of the school board and their supporters in their continual effort to put a new high school building project before the voters, was, from the perspective of the new school proponents, an act of loyalty to the majority in the town who had been turning out and voting for it year after year (the measure needed 60 percent support to pass).

The important point to note is that the willingness to listen to each other empathetically and bring their assumptions into the open without judgment, led to breakthroughs that freed the group's creativity and unleashed members of each side from their habitually held and embattled positions. This disciplined process of dialogue became the path to new solutions and insights that were grounded in the combined experience of the whole community. The result was a kind of "public knowledge" that was generated, which became the basis for moving forward.

After meeting for four months, the group issued a report, a summary of which was published in the local newspaper that, interestingly enough, stated many points on which the group had reached some consensus. One of the surprising results of their deliberations was that they did not recommend any particular plan for a new school. Instead, they offered a set of meaningful insights that they hoped would complement the school board's future efforts when preparing a proposal for updating and expanding the cooperative school facilities.

The common ground insights emphasized the dire need to improve the existing school district's facilities, the need to reduce what had been the cost estimates heretofore for a new school, the importance of maintaining the existing high school site for the well-being of the town of Jaffrey, and the recommendation that the school board develop a long-term plan for addressing the needs from kindergarten through high school over the next 20 years. Finally, they underscored the need for better communication between the school board and citizens in each town about future plans.

The effect of these outcomes was a message to the school board and other officials to stop pushing for a new school as the only solution to the district's educational needs. After months of ongoing dialogue, the group saw the problem as more complicated and in need of a more modest, incremental, and multifaceted set of solutions. The school board and its facilities and planning subcommittee balked at first to this group's recommendations but in the end accepted them and used their insights and recommendations to build a new multiphased approach to school improvement to be put to the voters over the next several years.

> *"A better answer to American individualism than what the communitarians were saying about returning to common beliefs and values, it seemed to me, was to ground our community-building and political practice on both the norms of public virtue and the practices of dialogue and deliberation. This, I believed was more appropriate to a modern, pluralistic society."*
>
> ("The Work of 'Public-Making': An interview with Douglas Challenger," *HEX*, 2004.)

The first phase of the school board's plan for facilities improvement was proposed in 2005 and was successful at the polls. Phase two, which included a $9.45 million bond for substantial renovations to the existing high school and middle school campus, also passed by a narrow margin in March 2006.

It's clear that over the past few years the Jaffrey-Rindge Cooperative School District has experienced the reversal of a long trend of deepening community conflict and continual electoral defeats for increased local funding for schools. What's more, is that even though the victories for school facilities improvements have been by narrow electoral margins, they have occurred without the same kind of divisiveness that was evidenced in the earlier years when citizens formed themselves into camps and traded insults in the local newspaper and at public meetings, and the resulting gridlock obstructed any major change from occurring.

Superintendent O'Neill said of the March 2006 election result, "It's nothing but good news." A selectman and member of the school board's facilities and planning committee said, "The logjam of our school facilities has been broken: we can now move on and fix our schools. Everyone came together and we found a compromise both communities could support." Privately, he told Drouin that this recent electoral success for the school board had its roots in the Citizens Seeking Common Ground initiative. "You and that group of citizens should feel very proud today," he said.

This story illustrates the importance of a public for healthy public institutions like schools. This group of citizens in the sustained dialogue became the nucleus for the public to move down the more productive path of working together. Through this process and their willingness to reach across their differences and self-interests for the good of the whole, the citizens were able to chart a direction for the school board to follow that could now be embraced and supported.

A Town/Gown Partnership Grows

Breaking the logjam began with that NIF forum on public schools held at Franklin Pierce University where a school administrator got a glimpse of "a different kind of talk, and another way to act," as the NIF slogan goes. But that forum was one small event in a previous three-year civic-engagement project that NECCL co-led called Rindge 2020, which used NIF-style processes to help the town map and discuss its future. Citizens from Rindge worked together with college students and faculty associated with that project. The project had a budget for inviting speakers to come make presentations on various problems that the town was facing. One of the Rindge 2020 subgroups working on the future of public education decided to hold an NIF forum instead of inviting an expert to the community to make a presentation.

Their decision to hold a participatory, citizen-based discussion was a pivotal moment, we thought, in the Rindge 2020 project, when citizens realized that *they* had the answers to their own local problems and had grown to trust deliberative community dialogue as a way to access their own collective wisdom. Years later that realization has continued to bear fruit, as one of the important links in the chain of public-building moments that has contributed to the health and democratic vitality of this region.

NECCL's involvement in projects like the Jaffrey-Rindge Study Circles project, the deliberative community forums of Rindge 2020, and the Citizens Seeking Common Ground sustained dialogue group has helped facilitate citizen creativity and cooperation among the neighboring communities and between them and Franklin Pierce University. Through this outreach and the public scholarship of faculty associated with these projects, the center has become a respected resource for the public work of the local towns and is increasingly looked to for advice and help as a community partner. This partnership has been recently engaged again to help address another community concern—the future of a well-loved memorial park in Rindge, called Cathedral of the Pines.

Over the last couple years, the Cathedral's board of trustees has been worried about the declining use of the memorial and its lack of appeal to younger generations. The center was sought to help the board think through their options and to address this issue in a public way, as the trustees see the memorial as a community possession rather than a private operation. Doherty and FPU history professor Mary Kelly have worked with the trustees to design class projects in which students research and present various future options, based on their conversations with the trustees. In the spring of 2006, several community forums were held to seek the ideas and deliberative wisdom of townspeople with regard to the various approaches the FPU students and faculty have designed.

The result was some clear direction for the future and a stronger relationship between the university and this cherished community asset. The consensus that emerged from these public sessions was a desire to see this former war-related memorial become a center for the study and promotion of peace, a substantial shift in the Cathedral's historical mission and operation. Plans are moving forward to hire its first executive director to bring this new vision into reality. In addition, townspeople and trustees of the Cathedral are hopeful that this new direction be carried out in relationship with Franklin Pierce University.

Civic Renewal and Building a Connecting Culture

The New England Center for Civic Life is part of the larger civic renewal movement of recent decades dedicated to community building and democracy in the United States. At the heart of the civic renewal movement is an emphasis on citizen-based politics that can complement and challenge the workings of formal government. This movement is unique in that, in large part, it has broken away from the politics of advocacy that characterized earlier grassroots movements and is instead animated by the idea of open and inclusive dialogue that takes into account diverse perspectives and tries to establish common ground among competing groups upon which workable compromises and approaches to public problems can be built.

> *"I wanted our college to offer the possibility for more faculty to redefine their professional lives."*
>
> ("The Work of 'Public-Making': An interview with Douglas Challenger," *HEX,* 2004.)

It is part of a new cultural paradigm for thinking about politics and political action that cuts across ideological lines and offers an alternative to "politics-as-usual." It represents a shift from what sociologist Philip Slater calls a "control culture" to a "connecting/ integrative culture." The older control culture is characterized by a set of assumptions that see the world as static matter, split into competing and warlike opposites, authoritarian, hierarchical, and changeable only through force and coercion. The new connecting culture that Slater sees emerging views the world as an energy process, an undivided whole, democratic, egalitarian, cooperative, and changeable through communicative processes that spawn spontaneous evolution.[1]

Another aspect of the civic renewal movement is the attempt to bring this understanding of connecting culture to young people through new kinds of civics education. While continuing to teach students the structure and workings of formal government, this movement emphasizes the role of civil society and the work of citizens in grassroots efforts to address issues in ways that spring

---

[1] Philip Slater, "Temporary Insanity: A World In Transition." http://www.philipslater.com (accessed August 2, 2007).

from their pragmatic experience and collective imagination, bear more public ownership and responsibility, and that complement official political processes and decision making.

The New England Center for Civic Life is seeking ways to teach, learn, and practice the principles of the new connecting culture. Now in its ninth year, the center has had considerable experience with that effort and has earned a reputation for offering a fresh approach to politics on and off campus and to civic learning within higher education. The early chapters of that story of achievement have been told in the pages of several issues of the *Higher Education Exchange*, but other exciting chapters are unfolding. The years ahead seem promising also because of the recent arrival of a new provost, the fourth chief academic officer of the university since the center's founding in 1998, who is enthusiastically supportive of the center's academic mission.

Coming of Age in New England

In the last few years, the center has deepened and extended its impact. Interestingly enough, this greater effectiveness seems to have come from a sharper focus on working more locally in our neighboring communities of Rindge and Jaffrey, and within the constraints of our institutional home of higher education and our professional lives as university teachers. This focus "closer to home," so to speak, was in part a function of accepting our limits of energy, time, and ability, especially in light of our heavy teaching loads at Franklin Pierce. At its inception, NECCL aspired to change the political culture and the civic education of students of New Hampshire and the New England region and to do what we could for those causes nationally. Looking back, this now appears a bit grandiose (and exhausting), even if it did seem at the time like a necessary part of the larger vision that helped inspire the founding of the center.

The question we asked ourselves in recent years, however, always seemed to be, how is what we are doing, or considering doing, helping our students? If we couldn't involve students in our activities, then, meaningful as the project might be, we had to decline being involved. Once Doherty became the director in the summer of 2003, she emphasized the center's academic identity and made sure that its resources focused on the application of deliberative dialogue to teaching and learning. This guiding academic imperative moved the center to focus more on its projects within the university and with other institutions of higher education with which we had made mentoring commitments, and less on public-building projects in communities and towns across the state. Any work off-campus had to be carefully circumscribed in terms of how much energy and time could be given by center personnel such as the rather low-level commitment that was involved with the Citizens Seeking Common Ground sustained dialogue in the Jaffrey-Rindge School District, or else it needed to involve students as has been the case in the Cathedral of the Pines project in Rindge.

This new geographically local, higher education specific, and professionally related focus has led to initiatives that have enhanced and enriched the ways we use deliberative dialogue on campus and in our teaching. As new faculty like Zan Goncalves, Molly Haas, and Heather Tuillio became attracted to the theory and practices of issue framing and deliberative dialogue, they brought this new pedagogy into their courses in both their academic disciplines and in the general education classes they taught. Their contributions have helped us learn how to better prepare students for more effective participation in forums through more concentrated study of content associated with the forum topic or through the use of panel discussions comprised of people telling their personal narratives that connect them and the student audience to the public issues being discussed.

Over time, the veteran center faculty like Donna Decker, Mary Kelly, Jed Donelan, and Doherty have improved how they organize deliberative dialogue activities and debrief them afterwards to enhance the learning experience of our students. And every year these faculty members mentor a group of approximately 10 students —Civic Scholars—with whom they work closely to plan and execute the many educational programs of the center. This past year's Civic Scholars, all of whom have been involved for almost their entire four years, were among the best students at the university, receiving honors in their major fields of study and recognized for their enormous civic contributions to campus life.

In addition to engaging a large proportion of our freshman class in campus forums each year through the freshman seminar and the center's leading program—the Diversity and Community Project, now upper-class students have opportunities to revisit these processes in a number of upper division general education courses and in several courses in various majors. We have also learned that we can sometimes be more successful engaging politically disinterested students through deliberative dialogues when we begin with more concrete and personal issues before we ask them to use the process with larger national and global topics, which seem more abstract to them. And as has always been the case, we continue to use issue framing in various courses as a way to teach disciplinary content as well as how to better understand and appreciate the perspectives of others. This new experimentation and experience with ways to use these practices in our courses has led to many innovations in the teaching of writing, media communications, ethics, history, sociology, American studies, and women's studies. Faculty and students alike, who are associated with the center, also find working together on common projects to be more personally fulfilling than more solitary forms of teaching, scholarship, and learning.

Presenting and Publishing the Center's Work

With the encouragement of our new provost, Michael Bell, the center's steering committee decided to begin gleaning what we have learned recently and over the course of the center's existence with the intention of writing a book together for the higher education community that will share with others the rewards and challenges of our combined experience. This plan to write, present, and publish what will soon be a decade of experience integrating the practices of deliberative democracy into our teaching and professional lives seems particularly appropriate at this time, as several grants that have sustained the center's work since the beginning have recently reached their end. "It is a good time to pause and take stock of our successes," said Doherty, "and to tell others what we have done and learned."

The goal to publish and present the center's work is part of affirming its identity as an academic institute as well as recognizing and accepting that the center is increasingly being asked by other colleges and universities to help strengthen their institutional efforts in diversity and civic education. Some of the institutions that have sought our consultation and training have included the University of New Hampshire, the University of Massachusetts-Boston, Bates College, Champlain College, Middlebury College, Woodbury College, and the State University of New York at Geneseo, among others. A book that highlights our best practices will be particularly useful for the center's growing role as consultants within higher education.

The new emphasis on publishing our work is taking another form currently in a new College Issues Forums series of issue books. These are modeled after the NIF booklets, but are discussion guides that have been developed at Franklin Pierce, which have grown out of our workshops and courses. They are written and illustrated in a style that has appeal to college-age students, and, in many cases, are focused on topics that are relevant to their lives in more immediate ways, such as the one entitled *Sex, Alcohol and a Million Decisions*. Other issue books that are currently being produced for this series are on topics such as gender, same-sex partners, socioeconomic class, religion and public life, and a discussion guide for teaching history on the Kansas-Nebraska Act of 1854.

The newly produced guide entitled *God and the Commons: Does Religion Matter?* will be used in spring 2007 in a statewide series of community forums which are part of a larger public engagement project on religion and public life, sponsored by the New Hampshire Humanities Council. In addition to providing a key discussion guide, the center has served as a consulting partner in this Humanities Council project.

Making a Place for Public Scholarship

So it seems that the New England Center for Civic Life is in a period of ripening and bearing the fruit of its first decade of work. This "fruit," in the form of a variety of publications, presentations, and consultations, will no doubt establish for it an even wider and more esteemed reputation as a leader in deliberation, dialogue, and civic-engagement processes in higher education. Interestingly enough, people at other institutions who have steadily turned to us for training and consultation from the time the center was first established have more easily recognized the value of the center's work than folks at our own university. Maybe it is simply a matter of the old saying that "a prophet in his own town is without honor."

Whatever the case may be, NECCL does seem to have finally earned a recognized place at the university even if its work is still understood by most of the faculty as peripheral to the main task of the traditional teaching of general education and disciplinary knowledge. This seemed to be the message in a recent discussion and refusal by the faculty union to *reject* an administrative proposal to make institute/center directors full-time *faculty* members, which would have better integrated the center and the other institutes into the mainstream life of the university. Still, faculty members who cite their work with the center are given credit for it in our university's promotion process. Service- and civic-learning projects that faculty design with students are increasingly seen as valuable ways to teach and are rewarded for such innovations in review processes.

NECCL's deeper institutionalization at Franklin Pierce University can be seen in a number of other ways, too. For example, for some time now the center has been advertised as one of the university's flagship programs in promotional publications and in any new academic job announcements published in regional newspapers or the employment sections of professional newsletters and in the *Chronicle of Higher Education*. Several new faculty members have been attracted to the university on that basis, and a few who have been hired in recent years have become deeply involved with the center. One of the goals of the new provost search committee was to hire a person who had good ideas about how to better integrate the new centers and institutes into the academic life of the university, which seemed to signal a certain degree of institutional acceptance.

After a particularly rough period a few years ago when faculty and administrative communication reached a crisis, the faculty realized that parliamentary procedure isn't always the best way to talk about controversial institutional defining issues, so they instituted a "deliberative" session as a standard part of the monthly faculty meetings. This choice to use deliberative dialogue as a form of communication when needed was clearly the result of NECCL's presence on campus. Also, FPU's new graduate program in leadership has sought to include the center in discussions of its curricular program and internships, and a certificate program that makes use of the community dialogue processes taught at the center is currently being discussed.

But, most telling of all, perhaps, was the recent decision of the university's board of trustees and president to ensure the future sustainability of the center by guaranteeing baseline funding for it out of the operational budget of the university. This means that the center's existence is no longer entirely dependent on the "soft" money of grants and contracts it secures. And additionally, the provost recently made the NECCL director's job a full-time administrative position.

Narrowing the Gap between the World It Is and the World It Should Be

With that as the case, we can look forward to even greater achievements in the future from the New England Center for Civic Life—this little school of democratic citizenship that is now stitched into the fabric of this university and this local community. The students who pass through our university and come into contact with the center and its programs are given a taste of this new connecting culture that will hopefully become a stronger part of political life in America, replacing the old, dysfunctional control culture, which dominates so much of the social landscape now.

The contrast of these two cultures reminds me of what one of NECCL's first student Civic Scholars said to me a year after she had graduated in 1999 and was working as a staffer in the U. S. Senate Majority Leader's office. She said that working with the center creating and leading community dialogues on campus was the highlight of her university experience. But, she went on to exclaim, "It is not at all how things work in Washington, D.C.!" In that student's mind, there was clearly a chasm between the world as it is and the world as it should be.

It's a gap also recognized by one of the adult participants in the Citizens Seeking Common Ground sustained dialogue group in the Jaffrey-Rindge School district when she reflected on her experience with these words, "What we have done here, as a group, is a lesson in how the world should work." With patience, creativity, and persistence, the New England Center for Civic Life is trying to narrow that gap, if only by helping some people see there is another way.

CHAPTER SIX

Democracy's Megachallenges Revisited

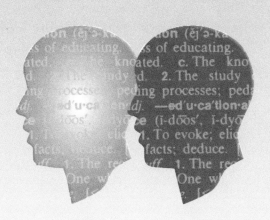

Democracy's Megachallenges Revisited

David Mathews

We are living in the midst of a contest over which kind of democracy will shape the 21st century. The dominant form of democracy in the last century was based primarily on elections and representative government. This system is in trouble today. The scholarly literature tells the story: *Democracy and Disagreement*; *Demosclerosis*; *Democracy's Discontent*; *Democracy at Risk*; and *Downsizing Democracy*.[1] All of these studies report that democracy is facing fundamental megachallenges.

Citizens know something is wrong, although they aren't sure what it is. In the United States, confidence in government dropped precipitously in the 1970s and has remained low ever since. In response, civic organizations have launched campaigns to "take the system back." A public engagement initiative has been joined by a civil renewal movement. Each reform has brought with it an implicit notion about what democracy should mean. But the notions are different.

Where does higher education stand in all this ferment? This essay addresses that question; it is about the megachallenges and their implications for everything from research and teaching to student services. Some universities have announced that they are "engaged" universities or colleges; others seem uncertain whether

---

[1] Amy Gutmann and Dennis Thompson, *Democracy and Disagreement* (Cambridge, MA: Belknap Press of Harvard University Press, 1996); Jonathan Rauch, *Demosclerosis: The Silent Killer of American Government* (New York: Random House, 1994); Michael J. Sandel, *Democracy's Discontent: America in Search of a Public Philosophy* (Cambridge, MA: Belknap Press of Harvard University Press, 1996); Stephen Macedo et al., *Democracy at Risk: How Political Choices Undermine Citizen Participation and What We Can Do About It* (Washington, DC: Brookings Institution Press, 2005); and Matthew A. Crenson and Benjamin Ginsberg, *Downsizing Democracy: How America Sidelined Its Citizens and Privatized Its Public* (Baltimore, MD: Johns Hopkins University Press, 2002).

they can or should do much about how the political system operates. Nonetheless, almost everything these institutions do, whether they say they are engaged or not, has implications for politics. The *Higher Education Exchange* is in a position to explore this issue further by looking at both what is going on in democracy and what is happening in higher education.

In this concluding chapter, I'll offer my reflections on what is occurring outside the academy and what it might mean for the way colleges and universities meet their responsibilities to democracy. I am returning to a subject I wrote about for the 1999 issue of the *Exchange* on the megachallenges of democracy. At that time, I had little to say about how higher education might respond. Now, I want to revisit these challenges and say more about the way colleges and universities might engage them.

How academic institutions go about meeting their obligations to democracy is crucial. I have heard it argued that these institutions serve democracy simply by existing. But what understanding of democracy does that argument imply? It seems rather limp given the current debate over what concept of democracy will emerge in the 21st century. The key question in that debate seems to be what role citizens will play. This question makes the issue of where the academy stands critical because colleges and universities have an understanding of citizenship that is implicit in nearly everything they do, including the kind of education they provide to undergraduates, the kind of leadership they champion in leadership programs, and the services they offer to their communities.

Determining the academy's position on citizenship, however, is no easy matter. There are so many groups involved—faculty, students, administrators, alumni, and trustees. But what institutional leaders say in their conferences and publications is revealing. Little of what they discuss has to do with democracy, at least directly. The topics are familiar: costs, academic standards, fundraising, athletics, enrollment trends. Some of the issues are, however, more political: affirmative action, diversity, multiculturalism, race, free speech, and equity. And there are some fairly new subjects in the literature that also have political overtones.

Service learning leads the list, followed by civic engagement and community involvement.

Obviously, all of the political topics have implications for democracy, but the implications are different. Within the mix are a wide range of notions about self-government, its problems, and the role of citizens. In the 2006 issue of the *Higher Education Exchange*, for instance, Derek Barker identified five quite distinct understandings of democracy all grouped under one generic label—the scholarship of public engagement.[2] I am not suggesting that there is anything wrong with this variety; as has often been said, one of the characteristics of democracy is a lively debate over its meaning. I don't expect the academy to speak with one voice or take one position in the contest over what democracy should mean. Nonetheless, it would be instructive if the concepts of democracy implicit in the various political projects of the academy were made more explicit.

I say this because I believe, at some point, the debate over the nature of democracy will subside and one form or another will become dominant. Its reign may last for some time, and it will determine the role that the public is to play in politics: citizens will either be in the front ranks or on the margins. Some types of democracy promote self-rule and rely heavily on citizens; others are more institutional or procedural and expect far less of citizens. The generation reading these issues of the *Exchange* could be held accountable for what is decided. It would be exceedingly unfortunate if future generations found ours wanting because we were not sensitive to the effects that academic projects are having on the prospects for self-rule. Our discussions of higher education should be informed by what is happening to democracy, both in the United States and around the world. What is happening in attempts at self-rule in communities is particularly important to understand. Communities can provide opportunities for people to learn to be citizens by participating directly in collective decision making and problem solving.

---

[2] Derek Barker, "Five Emerging Practices in the Scholarship of Engagement," *Higher Education Exchange* (2006): 64-72.

The true measure of the *Exchange*'s significance will be how deeply it delves into the problems of democracy and how explicitly it lays out the implications of those problems for colleges and universities. To the credit of its editors and authors, *HEX* has already added some important insights to the current debate, discussing concepts such as "public building," "public work," and "public scholarship." These concepts have developed as democratic theory has been combined with academic practice. (Several of those who have introduced these notions have elaborated on what they mean in this book.)

The repeated reference to the "public" in these concepts is significant because of the questions surrounding the role of citizens in a democracy. The word *public* can have a variety of meanings. For instance, many of these new concepts seem to refer to a single public. That is interesting because most people don't refer to the public in the singular today; they speak of publics, meaning particular groups with a common interest or identity. This concept of multiple publics is consistent with the nature of the current political system, which is built around a greatly expanded constellation of increasingly powerful interest groups. Yet references to new movements, which range from public librarianship to public journalism, suggest that we are rethinking the nature of democracy. To speak of "the public" seems to return to an earlier notion of democracy when the sovereign authority was "the People," a diverse but coherent body politic. We need to know more about how these movements understand "the public." Is more implied than in "public" restrooms or "public" transportation, which is simply everyone or the total population?

These movements (public history is another) are within disciplines, and they coincide with institutional initiatives to reengage citizens or serve the communities where colleges and universities are located. Such outreach efforts have attracted a considerable following on campuses. Unlike the 1970s, when something similar was attempted, there now appears to be more faculty support. In fact, many of the public initiatives are coming from faculty groups (at Penn State, for instance) or even from faculty senates (at the

University of Minnesota, for example). Having been invited to several of these faculty discussions, I have been impressed by their potential to explore the kinds of democracy that are implied by various outreach initiatives.

Whether or not it is intentional, there will be some impact from these academic initiatives. In their book tracing the growth of faculty power on campuses in the 1960s and 1970s, Christopher Jencks and David Riesman note that the redistribution of power brought on by the professionalization of the faculty resulted in "the promotion of meritocratic values" both inside and outside the academy.[3] This was not the result of a conscious decision by the academy, but it happened. So the question of which political values are implicit in the current outreach efforts is inescapable.

To accomplish what I hope to in this essay—to explore the implications for colleges and universities of the major problems in contemporary democracies—I have selected current political trends that raise troubling questions about the future of self-rule, which is the definition of democracy that I use. (Self-rule, wonderfully described by Robert Wiebe in a book by that name, came to define the American political system that developed on the early 19th-century frontier—despite the late 18th-century's preference for a republic of representative government and not a democracy.)[4]

The first trend on my list is one that affects the communities where colleges and universities are located. Towns and cities are plagued by problems that grow out of the lack of a sense of community and then further rend the social fabric. These have been called "wicked" problems and were discussed in the 1999 issue of *HEX*.

A problem is wicked when the diagnosis or definition is unclear, the location or cause is uncertain, and any effective action

---

[3] Christopher Jencks and David Riesman, *The Academic Revolution* (1968; repr., New Brunswick, NJ: Transaction Publishers, 2002).

[4] Robert H. Wiebe, *Self-Rule: A Cultural History of American Democracy* (Chicago: University of Chicago Press, 1995).

to deal with it requires narrowing the gap between what is and what ought to be—in the face of disagreement about the latter.[5] Wicked problems are more human than technical and are so deeply embedded in the social fabric that they never completely go away. They are as tricky as they are aggressive. Each symptom exposes another problem in a never-ending chain.

Given these characteristics, conventional strategies of goal setting, planning, and evaluation aren't enough. When problems are wicked, a shared understanding of the nature of what people are confronting is more important than an immediate solution. In fact, dealing effectively with a wicked problem may depend on not reaching a decision about a solution early on. The ability of citizens to exercise sound judgment in the face of uncertainty is especially critical! No one group of stakeholders nor single institution can solve problems with these characteristics. These problems can't be managed unless there is a collective public that acts in a community—and keeps on acting —through a series of richly diverse initiatives.

Wicked problems challenge institutions of higher education that want to assist communities because the things the institutions normally provide, such as expertise and technical assistance, aren't always useful in addressing these deeply embedded problems, which often defy professional solutions. Some institutions now make a distinction between providing community assistance without due regard for what people say they need and providing service based on some locally defined need. And some professionals describe themselves as the "guide on the side" rather than the "sage on the stage." The critical question, however, is what the professional on the side does with problems that can't be solved by professional expertise.

In the 2005 issue of *HEX*, Christa Slaton described an Auburn University project that spoke to this question. Rather than offering solutions, she and her colleagues decided to use their expertise to help a community build the civic capacity to combat its wicked problems.[6]

---

[5] The classic reference on wicked problems is Horst W. J. Rittel and Melvin M. Webber, "Dilemmas in a General Theory of Planning," *Policy Sciences* 4 (1973): 155-169.

[6] Christa Daryl Slaton, "The University Role in Civic Engagement: Serving as a Spark to Community-Building," *Higher Education Exchange* (2005): 34-42.

Similar cases have also been reported in the *Exchange*. In all of them, the projects had to go beyond providing services to develop an engagement strategy that took into account the nature of wicked problems.

In the community that Slaton wrote about, economic decline and an increase in drug-related crime had devastated a rural town. The town had already been inundated with technical assistance from nearby institutions. But as soon as the service providers returned to their campuses, local people returned to business-as-usual. Slaton described what she and her colleagues did to break this pattern. First, they recognized that the problems were wicked enough that they required the "whole village" to respond; that is, they required citizens to work together to do things that no one else could do for them. That recognition informed the university's engagement strategy. The academics backed off from offering technical assistance and proposed that citizens meet, decide what they wanted to do to revive their community, and act on what they decided. The group from Auburn offered information when asked but stayed on the sidelines so citizens could take over the playing field. My brief account doesn't do justice to all the knowledge and skill that faculty members brought to the project, but it does show that they succeeded in breaking the old pattern; citizens did not fall back on old habits when the Auburn representatives left.

Most engagement initiatives involve just one center or department, so it will be interesting to see whether these projects bring about any changes in their university's approach to service. Will the politics implicit in Auburn's strategy prompt an intrauniversity examination of the kind of politics implicit in conventional outreach efforts? It will be particularly interesting to see whether the new engagement projects affect student community-service programs, which are typically based on traditional models of university assistance.

Another troubling trend affecting democracies is the propensity for moral disagreements to polarize representative governments or, in some cases, degenerate into violence. One of the most sobering realizations of the late 20th century has been that political systems based on contested representation, that is, those that rely primarily on elections and representative assemblies, are not always effective in dealing with moral disagreements. These disagreements have split the U.S. political system into rigid camps of red and blue, and they are inflaming other countries as well, especially in the Middle East. Moral disagreements are to be expected in politics, particularly democratic politics, because the issues are fundamentally about what should be. Resolving disagreements by bargaining among partisans is difficult, especially when the disagreements are based on deeply held convictions. And as Amy Gutmann and Dennis Thompson have pointed out, "the standard theories of democracy —proceduralism and constitutionalism … are surprisingly silent about the need for ongoing discussion of moral disagreement in everyday political life."[7] They are among a number of scholars calling for a more deliberative understanding of democracy.

Deliberation in democracy takes into account the things people consider valuable (which are moral considerations). To deliberate is to decide by weighing options for action against what people hold dear. More is on the table than what is feasible or efficient from a technical point of view. Furthermore, the goal of democratic deliberation is not an absolute and immutable conclusion but a provisional decision about which direction to follow or purpose to serve. Being provisional, the decision is open to change as new circumstances dictate.

The question for higher education is how the various forms of democracy it supports, explicitly or implicitly, deal with the inevitability of moral disagreement. Universities have numerous programs in negotiation, mediation, and other conflict-resolution techniques. All to the good! But deliberative democracy requires more; it is not a technique, per se, for dealing with crises or disagreements. Deliberation creates a continuous conversation about what is most important to people in everyday life, which is morally grounded. It is a different way to do politics that puts citizens, not just stakeholders or combatants, at the center.

---

[7] Gutmann and Thompson, *Democracy and Disagreement*, 12.

In 2005, the *Exchange* reported on an experiment at Wake Forest University by two faculty members, Katy Harriger and Jill McMillan, who tested deliberative democracy as a way of doing politics. It was introduced at multiple sites: in classrooms, in the campus community, and in the town where the university is located. Deliberation was not presented as just a way of conducting forums, but instead as a way of living democratically. The initial report showed that this concept of politics challenges academic institutions at every level: from the very meaning of scholarship to the nature of teaching and the character of the extracurricular program. Harriger and McMillan found that deliberative democracy calls into question all the roles professors have become accustomed to as teachers, researchers, and even citizens. In fact, the project challenged the assumption that these are separate roles.

The impact that this experiment had on the cohort of students who participated (as compared to those who didn't) was significant. As one participant said, it affected everything she did. She and her classmates developed a different sense of democracy, especially an appreciation of the need for citizens to work together. Politics, the students found, involved more than electing representatives. And that understanding gave them an expanded sense of the many ways they could be effective political actors.[8]

Perhaps the greatest challenge that public deliberation poses for academe comes from its epistemological implications. Deliberation creates morally relevant, "public knowledge" about what is most important to people's collective well-being. This knowledge has to be socially constructed by citizens. It is neither better nor worse than expert, scientific knowledge, just different, as the theoretical literature has recognized for some time. So the goal of public knowledge (perhaps better called practical wisdom) is to generate sound judgments about what should be done in politics. How institutions

---

[8] Katy J. Harriger and Jill J. McMillan, "Public Scholarship and Faculty Role Conflict," *Higher Education Exchange* (2005): 17-23. The Kettering Foundation Press has recently published a book on this research, see Katy J. Harriger and Jill J. McMillan, *Speaking of Politics: Preparing College Students for Democratic Citizenship through Deliberative Dialogue* (Dayton, OH: Kettering Foundation Press, 2007).

of higher education contribute to this knowledge that people need to rule themselves wisely is an open question.

This is a question that faculty members have addressed, in what has been called "public scholarship." The term *public scholarship* has been taken as an implicit criticism of disinterested scholarship or as a call for social and politically relevant research that is popular and not critical of existing conventions. This isn't what public scholarship means to the faculty members that Kettering has been collaborating with. These academic members are raising different issues; they appreciate the importance of knowledge that is not immediately relevant and aren't playing to the grandstands. They recognize the difference between the kind of knowledge people use to make sound political judgments and the kind of knowledge academics produce, and they look for any useful relationship between the two.

A Danish social scientist, Bent Flyvbjerg, has an excellent piece in the 2002 issue of the *Exchange* on how scholars can assist in the social construction of political wisdom. This wisdom develops around these questions: 1) Where are we going? 2) Is this desirable? and 3) What should be done? (Those, not coincidentally, are the three primary questions in public deliberation.)[9]

Flyvbjerg proposes a type of social science that would complement public deliberation. His methodology anticipates moral disagreements by including what is often excluded in research—subjective experiences, local context, and human values (the things people care about). Most important, he allows for multiple descriptions of reality and the possibility of more than one valid interpretation. Conclusions would be reached through a dialogue among those affected by the research, citizens and scholars alike. It follows from this methodology, he argues, that scholars must work to improve the conditions under which the dialogues occur.[10] (That is exactly what the Auburn faculty did.)

---

[9] Laura Grattan, review of *Making Social Science Matter: Why Social Inquiry Fails and How It Can Succeed Again*, by Bent Flyvbjerg, *Higher Education Exchange* (2002): 51.

[10] Ibid., 49-53.

I don't know whether any of Flyvbjerg's ideas or his practical advice have been taken up by U.S. research universities. If they have, it would be more than just interesting to know the results. The closest I have seen is in the research being done at the Centers for Disease Control, where public deliberation has been used to shape policy on dealing with high-risk, unpredictable pandemics like avian flu.

Still another political trend, one that poses perhaps the ultimate threat to self-rule, is the tendency to "sideline citizens and privatize public life," a phrase used by two scholars, Matthew Crenson and Benjamin Ginsberg. They describe the numerous ways that have been devised to make a collective citizenry unnecessary:

> Political elites have found ways to achieve their policy objectives without mobilizing voters. Rather than take issues to the electorate for resolution, today's contending elites attempt to outdo their opponents by litigating, [or] by manipulating administrative procedures ... that remove policy to arenas beyond the reach of their rivals. In the process, the millions of citizens who might once have been called to the aid of their parties now remain passive bystanders. Yesterday's actors have become today's audience— spectators and customers rather than citizens.[11]

The mechanism for dislodging citizens may be the result of a widespread perception among leaders that "the people" are ineffective or simply inconvenient. As one civic leader told us about his community, "democracy just doesn't work here."

At best, as Crenson and Ginsberg note, citizens are treated as customers to be served. Their role is to choose, much as consumers would, from shelves of political leaders, policies, and government programs. This notion of the public, critics argue, privatizes citizens in a personal sort of democracy, which leaves no place for people to exercise their collective power in the interest of the polity as a whole. Power comes instead from the many publics that are formed

---

[11] Crenson and Ginsberg, *Downsizing Democracy*, 48.

around particular, rather than inclusive, interests. Governments are organized to bargain or negotiate with these interest groups.

This analysis suggests that the way academic institutions influence their students' understanding of their own citizenship is critical because of the contested notions of what citizens should do. What do colleges and universities have to say to people who feel they have been pushed out of their own political system, who feel that citizens-as-citizens have been marginalized?

A quick scan of the *Exchange*, including what I have written, didn't uncover any discussion of sidelining citizens. I was puzzled by what appeared to be a lack of attention to the most dangerous trend of all—a democracy without a public. Then I remembered that the *Exchange* had published articles on the role of professionals in democracy. And these articles addressed the role of citizens. In an August 1998 issue of the *Economist*, an article appeared that assessed the foundation's work in providing briefing books for citizens on major policy issues (the National Issues Forums series of issue books). The author of the article dismissed the foundation's efforts as naïve because, he argued, the modern world was managed by professionals. Citizens were helpless "amateurs" who could not possibly have sound opinions on any complex issue.[12]

The *Economist* article was extolling one of the forces that threatens to dislodge the public from its place as the final and sovereign authority in democracy: professionalism. The implication for higher education is obvious. Most professionals are trained in our colleges and universities. I suspect, however, that most professional schools wouldn't agree that they are part of a trend to push citizens to the sidelines. They would probably insist that what they teach is decidedly *not* political—including their courses on ethics. They have a point about not being political—but only in the narrow meaning of politics, which is restricted to electing representatives and making laws. Most individuals who become professionals aren't, in this sense, motivated by a political agenda; their goal is to become excellent in their field. We all appreciate a good physician or accountant,

---

[12] "Building the Perfect Citizen," *The Economist*, August 22, 1998, 21-22.

but the professionalism that the writer for the *Economist* was applauding is a different matter. It is based on the assumption that a small group of people, because they are scientifically trained, know what is best for all of us. As more and more fields have become professional domains, the contention that citizens don't count seems logical. Yet the conflict with democracy is inescapable. Democracies are based on the proposition that, collectively, we can make better decisions about our well-being than any one person or group of people.

The sidelining of citizens can occur in the most innocent way. For instance, professionals naturally give names to problems that reflect their expertise. That is their job, and we rely on their powers of diagnosis and the remedies they offer. But there can be unintended consequences. While professionals name problems in their terms, these terms don't necessarily resonate with the names citizens use. I recall Wendell Berry's story of an economist explaining that it was cheaper to rent land than buy it, only to be challenged by a farmer who pointed out that his ancestors didn't come to America to be renters.[13] The economist was technically correct, but the name of the problem wasn't just profitability. The farmer had additional concerns about maintaining a way of life he valued and the independence that owning land provided.

Even though professional names are accurate, they can be so expert that they create the impression that no other names are possible. When that happens, people don't see their worries reflected in the way problems are presented, so they back off. Furthermore, the solutions that are implicit in names may give the impression that there is little that citizens can do.

Recently, I was in a discussion about what New Orleans needed to do to recover from Hurricane Katrina. When I suggested that there were some things that only citizens could do, I was challenged with a comment to the effect that only the Corps of Engineers could rebuild the levees. I was struck by how easily a technical solution had come to define a much more complex problem and how that solution put citizens on the sidelines.

---

[13] Wendell Berry, *The Unsettling of America: Culture and Agriculture* (San Francisco: Sierra Club Books, 1986), viii.

I am not suggesting that professionals have to give up their way of describing problems, but they could recognize that the names citizens use are different—and valid. That recognition would help get citizens off the sidelines because people are engaged by names that reflect their experiences and concerns. As was true of the farmer, public names capture invaluable intangibles. For instance, crime can be described in statistical terms, but people value safety or being secure from danger. And there is no number, or measurement, that quantifies feeling secure.

I need to make two crucial distinctions here. First, naming a problem in public terms isn't the same as describing it in everyday language. Public terms identify what have been called primal motives or imperatives. These are the things people consider essential to their shared future, the very ends or purposes of life, and the means necessary for achieving those ends. Our collective or broadly political needs are similar to the individual needs that Abraham Maslow found common to all human beings.[14] Second, naming problems in public terms doesn't result in a one-dimensional description or a single name. A community will use many names because there is always more than one concern at stake.

The discrepancy between professional and public names for problems is a symptom of a more basic tension between the politics implicit in a professional culture and democratic politics. Bill Sullivan, writing for the *Exchange* in 1996, noted that, as professionalism has been increasingly identified with expert knowledge and technical solutions, citizens have seemed less and less competent. Consequently, moving them to the sidelines has made sense. Citizens, in response, have come to see professionals as insensitive and unaware of the things people hold dear. As a remedy, Sullivan advocates a more civic professionalism.[15]

Today, some professionals are becoming more civic and trying to reengage a democratic citizenry in their work. And they are

---

[14] Milton Rokeach and Sandra J. Ball-Rokeach, "Stability and Change in American Value Priorities, 1968-1981," *American Psychologist* 44 (May 1989): 775-784.

[15] William M. Sullivan, "The Public Intellectual as Transgressor?" *Higher Education Exchange* (1996): 17-22.

attempting to reconcile the professional tilt toward meritocracy with the values of democracy. The American Bar Association (ABA) is one example. They have prepared guides to stimulate public deliberation on issues that concern both lawyers and citizens.[16] These deliberations give the ABA insights into how citizens name problems. And citizens are drawn off the sidelines by having to make decisions about how to improve the judicial system.

I applaud civic professionalism because it recognizes the inevitable tensions in a society that is both professional and democratic (as ours is). But I doubt that it can be advanced by simply adding a course on the subject in every professional school. It might be more effective to provide students with civic experiences in associations trying to engage citizens. And academic institutions could do more to support scholars who are recovering the civic roots of their professions. There is an emerging literature to build on. For instance, Claire Snyder has written on the civic history of social science scholarship for the *Exchange,* and Scott Peters has a recently edited book that includes stories about the civic objectives of pioneers in public scholarship at state and land-grant institutions.[17]

Though not always tied to professional schools, new centers have developed on campuses around the country for the purpose of strengthening the ties between academic institutions and the democratic citizenry. And their efforts have been reported in the *Exchange.* More than 30 of these centers or institutes have been established on campuses to encourage the use of public deliberation, not only by professionals and associations but also by community groups.

The challenges facing democracy that I have cited are only three among many. I have concentrated on those that are fundamental; that is, those that affect the ability of democracy to function as it should. Because they damage the heart muscles of self-government,

---

[16] American Bar Association, *"… And Justice for All": Ensuring Public Trust and Confidence in the Justice System* (American Bar Association, 2001).

[17] R. Claire Snyder, "The Civic Roots of Academic Social Science Scholarship in America," *Higher Education Exchange* (2000): 5-16 and Scott J. Peters et al., eds., *Engaging Campus and Community: The Practice of Public Scholarship in the State and Land-Grant University System* (Dayton, OH: Kettering Foundation Press, 2005).

fundamental problems are different from the no-less-important circumstantial problems—poverty, natural disasters, and the like—that can plague democratic countries. Fundamental problems eventually make their way onto the pages of academic literature, and reading that literature is one way for institutional leaders to monitor the threats to democracy. I would suggest, however, that there are better, more direct ways. But these raise questions about where institutions and professionals should "stand" in a democratic society.

The drop-in, drop-out, observe, and advise relationship with communities is problematic. Institutions have to enter politics in a way that is consistent with the politics they want to promote. The drop-in strategy is more meritocratic than democratic. The embedded presence of various kinds of on-site or extension agents is potentially less meritocratic, depending, of course, on the way the agents behave. The embedded agent model certainly affords institutions direct contact with the people who are battling the threats to democracy. I said "people" and not institutions because institution-to-institution contacts already exist. Colleges and universities are often engaging local civic organizations when they say they are engaging communities. The people on the front lines fighting democracy's battles, however, are usually at the farthest outpost of these organizations or not in formal institutions at all. Granted, it is much more difficult to establish ties with the unorganized citizen than the organized; still, the front lines of democracy are typically being held by ad hoc associations, nameless groups, and an array of civic innovators.

Unfortunately, one group of ideally embedded agents seems to be relatively unengaged in response to the fundamental challenges facing democracy; these are the trustees of colleges and universities. They live in communities and are usually active in civic affairs. Apparently, many board members see their job as representing their institutions to the public more than the public to their institutions. Or if they represent the public, it is primarily to see that funds are well spent and laws are observed. I hope I am wrong about governing boards. We have seen a few trustees at meetings on the challenges of democracy, and the *Exchange* has published one interview on the subject with a trustee of the University of South Carolina.[18] But that is all we've seen.

There are numerous roles that citizen trustees could play in academic outreach. Trustees are certainly in a position to establish ties with the informal associations of citizens. And they are in a position to help connect their institutions' outreach projects to similar engagement efforts already going on in community groups, professional associations, regional organizations, government agencies, and legislative bodies. Colleges and universities that want to be more engaged might begin by engaging these fellow travelers.

As things stand now, the initiative for civic engagement is coming primarily from the faculty. They could use more administrative and trustee support. And they could benefit from ties to civic engagement efforts going on in organizations and ad hoc groups off campus. I say all of this with a sense of urgency because the stakes are high. The world is struggling with the meaning of democracy as current problems challenge old forms. Questions of where academic institutions will weigh in—and how—are inescapable. The way these questions are answered, knowingly or not, will be the ultimate measure of how accountable colleges and universities are to the public.

---

[18] "On the Role of Trustees: An interview with William C. Hubbard," interview by David Brown, *Higher Education Exchange* (2001): 38-42.

Contributors

Harry C. Boyte is the founder and codirector of the Center for Democracy and Citizenship and a senior fellow at the Humphrey Institute. His recent works include *Everyday Politics* (University of Pennsylvania Press, 2004) and *The Citizen Solution*, forthcoming from the Minnesota Historical Society and the Kettering Press. He was national coordinator of the national New Citizenship coalition, and is now helping to organize the Civic Field Project with the American Association of State Colleges and Universities.

David W. Brown is coeditor of the *Higher Education Exchange*. He taught at Yale's School of Management, New School's Milano Graduate School, and authored *When Strangers Cooperate* (Free Press, 1995), and *Organization Smarts* (Amacon 2002). He has also practiced law and served as a state commissioner, deputy mayor, public authority board member, and college president.

Douglas Challenger is professor of Sociology at Franklin Pierce University in Rindge, New Hampshire, where in 1998, he founded and directed, until 2003, the New England Center for Civic Life. As a Senior Fulbright scholar in Slovenia in 1996-1997, he studied Slovene approaches to civic education and lectured on social foundations of democracy. He has published a book on social theory and several articles on contemporary political thought and the application of deliberative dialogue practices in colleges and communities.

Jeremy Cohen is a professor of Communication at The Pennsylvania State University where he serves also as associate vice president and senior associate dean for Undergraduate Education. He developed and directs The Laboratory for Public Scholarship and Democracy and chairs the intercollege Bachelor of Philosophy program.

Peter Levine is director of CIRCLE (The Center for Information & Research on Civic Learning & Engagement), a member of the Kettering Foundation board, and author of five books, most recently *The Future of Democracy: Developing the Next Generation of American Citizens* (2007).

David Mathews, president of the Kettering Foundation, was secretary of Health, Education, and Welfare in the Ford administration and, before that, president of The University of Alabama. He has written extensively on education, political theory, southern history, public policy, and international problem solving. His books include *Why Public Schools? Whose Public Schools?* (NewSouth Books, 2003); For Communities to Work (Kettering Foundation, 2002); and a revised second edition of Politics for People (University of Illinois Press, 1999). His newest book focuses on the relationship between the public and public education: *Reclaiming Public Education by Reclaiming Our Democracy* (Kettering Foundation Press, 2006).

Noëlle McAfee is a visiting associate professor of philosophy at George Mason University and associate editor of the Kettering Review. She is the author of *Democracy and the Political Unconscious* (forthcoming 2008); *Habermas, Kristeva, and Citizenship; and Julia Kristeva*. She also coedited with James Veninga the book *Standing with the Public: the Humanities and Democratic Practice* and with Claire Snyder a special issue of the journal *Hypatia* on feminist engagements in democratic theory.

Scott J. Peters is associate professor in the Department of Education at Cornell University. His research is centered on a critical examination of the social, political, and cultural identities, roles, purposes, and work of academic institutions and professionals. He pursues his research in two related lines of inquiry: a historical line that focuses on the origins and early development of the national land-grant system's agricultural extension work, and a line that utilizes narrative inquiry to analyze and interpret the civic engagement experiences and public purposes and work of contemporary land-grant scholars and extension educators. A key theoretical and practical problem his research seeks to address is that of the dilemma of the relation of expertise and democracy in the academic profession.

R. Claire Snyder is director of academics for the higher education program and associate professor of political theory at George Mason University. Her publications include *Citizen-Soldiers and Manly Warriors: Military Service and Gender in the Civic Republican Tradition* (1999), *Gay Marriage and Democracy: Equality for All* (2006), and *"Feminist Theory and Democratic Thought"* (2007), a special issue of *Hypatia: Journal of Feminist Philosophy* (coedited with Noelle McAfee).

Mary Stanley taught at Syracuse University's Maxwell School of Citizenship and Public Affairs for many years. Currently she is an independent scholar, writer, and researcher. She has published in the areas of citizenship, service learning, and the role of women in public life. Mary was a founder/producer/host of the award-winning NPR affiliate WAER's, "Women's Voices Radio." Presently she is researching the role of cross-cultural democratic deliberation in sustainable community and economic development through the arts. Stanley lives in Parati, Brazil, and Syracuse, New York.

Adam Weinberg is provost and senior vice president for academic affairs at World Learning and the School for International Training. From 1994-2005, he was on the faculty at Colgate University where he served in a number of positions including Dean of the College. During this time, he worked and wrote extensively on how universities can be catalysts for social and economic development. In his new position with World Learning, Weinberg oversees efforts in more than 75 countries to connect education to social justice, equity, and human rights efforts.

Deborah Witte is coeditor of the *Higher Education Exchange* and a program officer with the Kettering Foundation. She is also a doctoral student in the Leadership and Change in the Professions program at Antioch University.